TEACHER EDITION

Merrill Physics

Principles and Problems

GLENCOE

Macmillan/McGraw-Hill

New York, New York Columbus, Ohio Mission Hills, California Peoria, Illinois

A Glencoe/McGraw-Hill Program

Merrill Physics: Principles & Problems

Student Edition
Teacher Wraparound Edition
Problems and Solutions Manual
Teacher Resource Package
Transparency Package
Laboratory Manual:
Student and Teacher Editions
Study Guide, Student Edition
Lesson Plan Booklet
English/Spanish Glossary
Computer Test Bank

These masters provide the structure of reviewing each major section of the chapter. Students will find these masters helpful in previewing and/or reviewing. The masters will prove helpful for preview at the time the chapter reading is assigned. The worksheets can be completed as the chapter is read and studied. All major concepts for each major section of the text are covered on these worksheets. When complete, the collection of these worksheets will prove to be an excellent review instrument.

ISBN 0-02-826739-7

Send all inquiries to: **GLENCOE DIVISION, Macmillan/McGraw-Hill**
936 Eastwind Drive
Westerville, Ohio 43081

Printed in the United States of America

3 4 5 6 7 8 9 MAL 99 98 97 96 95

Contents

Contents

DATE ________ PERIOD ________ NAME ________________________________

CHAPTER 1 Study Guide

Fill in the blanks as you study the chapter.

Physics: The Search for Understanding

Physics is the branch of knowledge that studies the ________ world. Scientists who work in this field are known as ________. They study the nature of ________ and ________, and how they are related. In their work, scientists try to find powerful ________ that describe more than one phenomenon, and lead to a better understanding of the ________. A(n) ________ is a framework of explanations hypothesizing how a discovery works. Physicists use ________ and ________ in developing theories. A theory can ________ experimental data and ________ results to new experiments. It can be developed before or after the results of ________ are seen. Physicists describe relationships, or ________, often using mathematics.

What and How, not Why: Scientific Methods

Aristotle and his followers made ________ of occurrences, and then used only ________ to draw conclusions. Galileo Galilei was one of the first European scientists to state that knowledge should be based on ________ and ________. Following Galileo's method of ________, ________, and ________, scientists approach problems in a(n) ________ way. Although the approach to the problem can vary, any organized approach is referred to as the ________. The results of experiments are carefully ________ because conclusions are drawn. Conclusions are then ________ further to see if they are valid.

DATE __________ PERIOD ________ NAME ______________________________

CHAPTER 2 Study Guide

Fill in the blanks as you study the chapter.

2.1 THE MEASURE OF SCIENCE

The Metric System

In the metric system, units of different sizes are related by ____________. The initials ______ stand for the International System of Units. The three fundamental units measure the quantities ______, ______, and ______. The meter is the SI unit of ______. The second is the SI unit of ______. The kilogram is the SI unit of ______. Other units are called derived units because they are ____________ of fundamental units.

Scientific Notation

Scientific notation is based on ____________ notation. In scientific notation, a measurement is expressed as a number between ______ and ______ multiplied by a whole-number ______ of ten. When numbers are converted to scientific notation, the decimal point is moved until there is one ________ digit to the ______ of the decimal point. The number of places the decimal point is moved is used as the ________ of ten. If the decimal point is moved to the ______, the exponent becomes larger. If the decimal point is moved to the ______, the exponent becomes smaller.

Prefixes Used with SI Units

SI units are changed by powers of ______ by the use of prefixes. The prefix for one tenth is ______. The prefix for one thousandth is ______. The prefix that changes a unit by one thousand is ______. All metric units use ________prefixes.

Arithmetic Operations in Scientific Notation

When numbers are in scientific notation, they may be added or subtracted if the numbers have the same ________. After the numbers are added, the exponent is ________. If the powers of ten are not the same, the ____________ must be moved, and the ________ must be changed before the numbers can be added. For multiplying numbers in scientific notation, the ________ do not have to be the same. After the numbers are multiplied, the exponents are ______ and the units are ________.

CHAPTER 2 Study Guide

NAME ______________________________

2.2 NOT ALL IS CERTAIN

Uncertainties of Measurements

A common source of error in making measurements comes from the _______at which the instrument is read. Parallax is the apparent change in _________ of an object when it is seen from different ________. Reading instruments at _______ level and ___________ reduces error due to parallax.

Accuracy and Precision

Precision is the degree of __________ to which the measurement of a quantity can be ____________. The precision of a measuring device is determined by the _______ division on its scale. Accuracy is the extent to which a measured value agrees with the __________ value of a quantity. Accuracy can be affected by changes in the ___________ used to make the measurement. Uncertainties in measurement affect __________ but not __________.

Significant Digits

In making measurements, there is a limit to the number of _______ that are valid. This limitation is caused by the __________ of the instrument used. The digits that are valid are called ___________ digits. The last significant digit in a measurement is a(n) _________, so it is __________. All __________ digits are considered to be significant. All final zeros ________ the decimal point are significant. Zeroes between two other significant digits _______ significant. Zeros used for spacing between significant digits and the decimal point _________significant.

Operations Using Significant Digits

The result of a mathematical operation with measurements cannot be more precise than the _______ precise measurement. When numbers are added or subtracted, the operation is performed first, and the answer is rounded off to correspond to the ____________ value involved. When numbers are multiplied or divided, the operation is performed first, and then the answer is rounded off to __________ number of significant digits as the factor with the _______ number of significant digits. Significant digits are used when calculating with ______________, but not when _________.

NAME ______________________________

2.3 DISPLAYING DATA

Graphing Data

When data are analyzed, the variable that is __________ is the independent variable. The dependent variables are the ______ of the independent variable. The __________ variable is plotted on the horizontal axis and the _________ variable is plotted on the vertical axis. After the dependent and independent variables have been identified, the ______ of each variable must be determined. It must be determined if the ______ is a valid data point. Each axis should be _________ and _______. Then the ______ are plotted and the ______ is drawn. Finally, the graph should be given a(n) ______.

Linear, Quadratic, and Inverse Relationships

The graph of a linear relationship is a(n) __________. The equation for such a relationship is __________. In this equation, m represents the ______ and b represents the _________. When one variable varies directly with the square of the other, the curve is in the shape of a(n) ________. The equation for such a curve is called a(n) _________ equation, and is written as ________. In this equation, k represents a(n) ________. In an inverse relationship, the curve is a(n) _________, and the equation that represents it is _________.

CHAPTER 2 Study Guide

NAME ________________________________

2.4 MANIPULATING EQUATIONS

Solving Equations Using Algebra

In manipulating equations, the relationship must not be ________. If one side of the equation is divided by a variable, the other side of the equation should be ________ by that variable. Any operation performed on one side of the equation must be ___________ the operation performed on the other side of the equation. If the equation for density, $D = m/V$, is solved for m, the correct equation is ________.

Units in Equations

Before mathematical operations are carried out, all terms in the equation must have _________ units. When an answer is written, it must include both the numerical ______ and the ______. If a term has several units, they are treated like any other mathematical ________.

DATE ________ PERIOD ______ NAME ____________________________

CHAPTER 3 Study Guide

Fill in the blanks as you study the chapter.

3.1 HOW FAR AND HOW FAST?

Position and Distance

An object's ________ can be described in terms of its relationship to a reference point. Choosing a reference point establishes a(n) ________ reference. Describing distance does not need a(n) ________ reference. Distance involves only a measurement of ________, and is a(n) ________ quantity. Position involves both ________ and ________, and is a(n) ________ quantity.

Average Velocity

If an object is moving, its position at one and only one time is a(n) ____________ position. The change in ________ of an object is its displacement, which is a(n) ________ quantity. The average velocity of an object is the change in ________ divided by the ____________ over which the change occurred. Average velocity is calculated using the equation ________. In this equation, ________, which is read as "delta *d*," stands for ____________. The symbol ________, which is read as "delta *t*," stands for ____________. Average velocity is expressed in a unit made up of a(n) ________ unit divided by a(n) ________ unit. Different units used to describe average velocity can be changed from one to another by the use of __________ factors.

Finding Displacement from Velocity and Time

Displacement can be calculated by using the equation __________. In this equation, ________ represents average velocity and ________ represents the time interval. If the average velocity of an object is the same at all ____________, the object is described as moving at constant, or ________, velocity. Constant velocity can be calculated using the equation ________.

Position-Time Graphs

A position-time graph is used to show how ________ depends on ________. If the motion is constant, the data produce a(n) ________ line, which means that the relationship between time and position is ________.

The Slope of a Position-Time Graph

On a position-time graph, the displacement is the ________ separation of two points. The time interval is the __________ separation. The slope of the line is the ratio of the ________ to the ________. The ________ of the line represents displacement. The ________ of the line represents the time interval. The slope of the line represents the ________ of the object.

CHAPTER 3 Study Guide

NAME ____________________

3.2 NEW MEANINGS FOR OLD WORDS

Positive and Negative Velocities

Displacements can be ________ or ________, but time intervals are always ________. Displacements to the ______ of the reference point are positive. Displacements to the ______ of the reference point are negative. Speed is the __________ of velocity. Speed is generally shown as positive, but velocity can be ________ or ________.

Instantaneous Velocity

If motion is not constant, the position-time graph does not produce a(n) ________ line. A straight line can be drawn ________ to the curve at any one point. The ______ of this line is the instantaneous velocity at that point.

Velocity-Time Graphs

In a velocity-time graph, ______ is shown on the horizontal axis and ________ is shown on the vertical axis. If velocity is constant, the velocity-time graph produces a(n) ________ line that is ________ to the horizontal axis. If velocity is increasing, the line has a(n) ________ slope. If velocity is decreasing, the line has a(n) ________ slope. The ________ value of any point on the line is the instantaneous velocity at that time. The area under the line on a velocity-time graph is equal to the __________ of the object from its original ________ to its ________ at a given time.

Relativity of Velocity

Measurements of ________ or ________ depend on the observer's frame of reference. If a person walks slowly toward the back of a moving train, an observer on the train would say that velocity and displacement are ________. An observer standing on the station platform would say that the walker's velocity and displacement are ________. However, when velocities approach the ____________, the frame of reference does not matter, and the velocity is _________. This concept is part of __________ theory of relativity.

DATE ________ PERIOD ________ NAME ____________________

CHAPTER 4 Study Guide

Fill in the blanks as you study the chapter.

4.1 WHAT IS ACCELERATION?

Average Acceleration

The change in ________ divided by the ____________ is average acceleration. It can be calculated using the equation __________. In this equation, _______ stands for acceleration, _______ stands for change in velocity, and _______ stands for the time interval. If velocity is measured in meters per second, acceleration is measured in _______, which is read as ____________________________. The unit also can be written as m/s^2, which is read as __________________________. Like velocity, acceleration is a(n) _______ quantity, which means it has both ___________ and _________. When velocity __________, acceleration is positive. When velocity ___________, acceleration is negative.

Average and Instantaneous Acceleration

A velocity-time graph shows how ________ depends on _______. The rise of the curve represents the change in ________. The run of the curve represents the ____________. The slope of the curve represents the ___________________. If the curve on a velocity-time graph is a straight line, the acceleration is _________. If the curve is not a straight line, acceleration is _________. The slope of a line tangent to the curve is the _________________________ at that time.

Velocity of an Object with Constant Acceleration

Acceleration that does not ________ in time is constant, or ________, acceleration. The velocity when the clock time is _______ is the initial velocity. The velocity after acceleration has occurred is called the _______ velocity, and is calculated using the equation _____________. In this equation, v_f is ____________, v_i is _____________, a is ____________, and t is _____________.

CHAPTER 4 Study Guide

NAME ______________________________

4.2 DISPLACEMENT DURING CONSTANT ACCELERATION

Displacement When Velocity and Time Are Known

If an object is accelerating, its displacement can be calculated using the equation ____________. In this equation, ______ stands for displacement, ______ stands for final velocity, ______ stands for initial velocity, and ______ stands for time interval. To find displacement using a __________ graph, find the area under the curve.

Displacement When Acceleration and Time Are Known

If initial velocity, acceleration, and time are known, the displacement of the object can be calculated using the equation ______________. In this equation, v_it stands for the ____________ of the object if it were moving at ________ velocity. In the equation, the term $\frac{1}{2}at^2$ stands for the __________ of the object starting from rest and moving with uniform __________. For an object accelerated from rest at a constant rate, the velocity-time graph produces a curve that is a(n) __________, and the position-time graph produces a curve that is a(n) ____________. If a line is drawn tangent to the curve of the position-time graph, the slope of that line is the ________________ at that point.

Displacement When Velocity and Acceleration Are Known

If initial and final velocities, as well as acceleration, are known, displacement can be calculated without using ______. The equation for this calculation is ____________. In this equation, d stands for ________, v_f stands for ___________, v_i stands for ___________, and a stands for __________.

Acceleration Due to Gravity

_______ was the first to show that all objects fall toward Earth with constant __________. The ______ of the object does not matter, as long as ___________ can be ignored. Acceleration due to gravity is represented by the symbol ______ . For an object falling downward, both _______ and __________ are negative. Acceleration due to gravity is equal to __________. As long as air resistance is ignored, the equations used involving acceleration can be used for falling objects if ______ is replaced by g. Because there are so many equations that can be used, it is important to read each problem carefully, and then identify the quantities that are ______ and the quantity that is ________. After an equation is selected, it may have to be ________ before the known values can be ________ in the equation.

DATE ________ PERIOD ______ NAME ______________________________

CHAPTER 5 Study Guide

Fill in the blanks as you study the chapter.

5.1 NEWTON'S LAWS OF MOTION

Forces

A force is a ______ or a ______. Because a force is a vector quantity, it has both magnitude and ________. Physicists group all forces into four kinds. They are ______________, ______________ ______, ________________, and __________. The weakest of the four forces is ______________. Charged particles cause the ____________ force to be exerted. The ___________ force is the strongest of the four forces, but only acts over small distances. The ______ force is involved in the radioactive decay of some nuclei. This force has been linked with the ____________ force.

Newton's First Law of Motion

Forces acting on an object can be _________ to produce the net force on the object. If all the forces acting in one direction are ________ all the forces acting on the object in the opposite direction, the net force is zero. According to ___________ law, if there is no net force on an object, the object remains at rest, or moves with ________ velocity in a _______ line.

Newton's Second Law of Motion

If there is a net force on an object, the object will be accelerated, or change _______. The amount of acceleration caused depends on the ______ of the force and the ______ of the object. Newton's second law can be written as an equation, ________. This equation means that acceleration is _______ proportional to force and ________ proportional to mass. The direction of the force and the direction of the acceleration are _________.

The Unit of Force

The unit of force is defined in terms of Newton's _______ law. The unit of force is the _______, abbreviated as ______. The amount of force that causes a mass of ___________ to accelerate at a rate of _________________________ is equal to one newton.

Newton's Third Law of Motion

Newton's third law describes pairs of forces called ____________ forces. These two forces are ______ in magnitude and ________ in direction. According to this law, if a book pushes downward on a table, the table pushes _______ against ________.

CHAPTER 5 Study Guide

NAME ________________________________

5.2 USING NEWTON'S LAW

Mass and Weight

An object's weight is the __________ force acting on the object. The unit used to express measurements of weight is the _______. Newton's _______ law can be used to find the weight of an object. The acceleration caused by gravity is equal to ________, and is represented by the symbol ______. The equation used for calculating weight is _______. According to the equation, an object's weight is proportional to its ______. An object's weight may vary from one location to another, because ____________________ may change from one place to another. However, the object's ______ does not change.

Two Kinds of Mass

One way to determine mass is to measure the amount of ______ needed to accelerate the object. This is called _______ mass. The other way to determine mass is to use a balance to compare the effects of __________ force on two objects. This is called __________ mass. In experiments, these two determinations of mass have been shown to be ______.

Friction

If you push on an object and slide it across a surface, the force of friction will _______ the motion. Friction acts in a direction that is _______ to the surface on which the object slides, and ________ to the direction in which the object slides. ______ friction opposes the start of an object's motion, and _______ friction opposes continuing the motion when the object is already in motion. Of these two forces, ______ friction is greater. The amount of friction can be calculated using the equation ________. The constant in the equation is called the ________________.

The Net Force Causes Acceleration

If more than one force acts on an object, the amount of acceleration can be calculated using Newton's _______ law. However, before the equation in Newton's law is used, the net force, which is the ______ of the forces, must be found. The positive and negative signs on the forces are important because they indicate the ________ of the forces.

The Fall of Bodies in the Air

Without any air, all objects fall with the same __________. When air is present, a friction-like force, called the _________, acts on the object. This force depends on the ______ and ______ of the object, the _______ of the air, and the ______ of motion. When this force is equal to the force of gravity, the net force on the object is ______, and the object has reached its ________ velocity.

DATE ________ PERIOD ________ NAME ______________________________

CHAPTER 6 Study Guide

Fill in the blanks as you study the chapter.

6.1 GRAPHICAL METHOD OF VECTOR ADDITION

Vector Addition in One Dimension

An arrow-tipped ____________ is used to represent a vector. To add two vectors, place the ______ of one vector at the ______ of the other vector, as shown below. The diagram represents an airplane flying east at 125 km/h. There is a 25.0-km/h tail wind. The long vector represents the velocity of the ________. The short vector represents the velocity of the ______. When adding these two vectors, the order of addition ______________. However, the ________ and the ______ of each vector must not be changed when drawn.

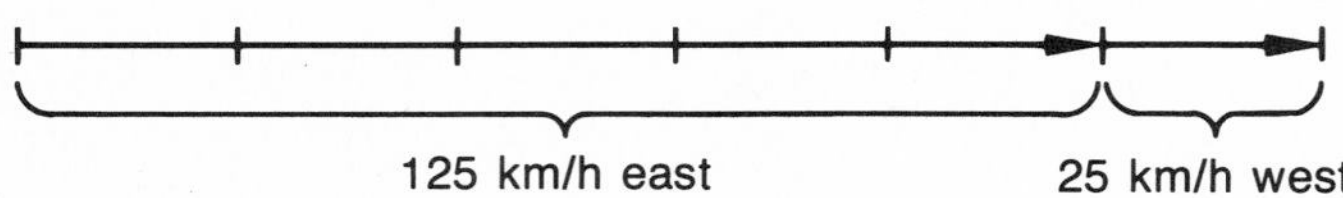

Vector Addition in Two Dimensions

When vectors in two dimensions are added, the ______ of one vector is placed at the ______ of the other vector, as shown below. The diagram represents an airplane flying east at 125 km/h. There is a 25.0-km/h cross wind blowing north. The long vector represents the velocity of the ________. The short vector represents the velocity of the ______. The resultant vector is drawn from the ______ of the first vector to the ______ of the second vector. The direction of the resultant is expressed as an angle measured ______________ from the ______.

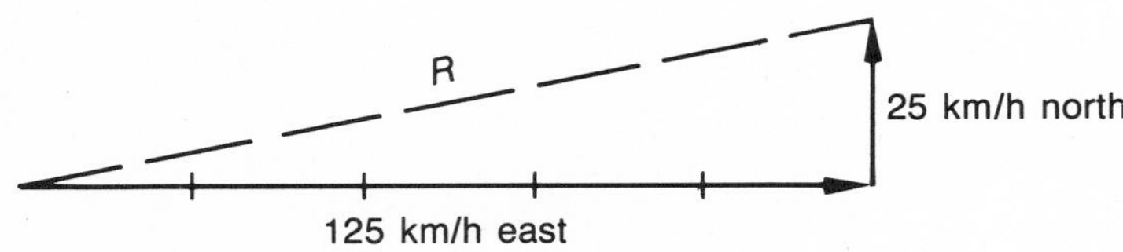

Addition of Several Vectors

When more than two vectors are added, the ______ in which they are added is not important. However, the ______ and ________ of each vector are important, and must not be changed. The diagram should show ______ vector for each force or motion involved.

Independence of Vector Quantities

The path of an airplane in a cross wind is determined by the airplane's own ________ and that of the wind. If the cross wind increases to 30.0 km/h, the wind vector and the ________ vector are changed, but the ________ vector is not changed.

CHAPTER 6 Study Guide

NAME ______________________________

6.2 ANALYTICAL METHOD OF VECTOR ADDITION

Adding Perpendicular Vectors

When two vectors are ____________, the vector diagram produces a right triangle, in which the resultant vector is the ____________ of the triangle. In the diagram below, an airplane flying east at 125 km/h is affected by a 25.0-km/h cross wind blowing to the north. The Pythagorean theorem can be used to calculate the ________ of the resultant vector. The equation to be used is ______________. The resultant is equal to __________. Trigonometry can be used to calculate the _________ the resultant. The equation used is ____________________, and the direction of the resultant is ______________.

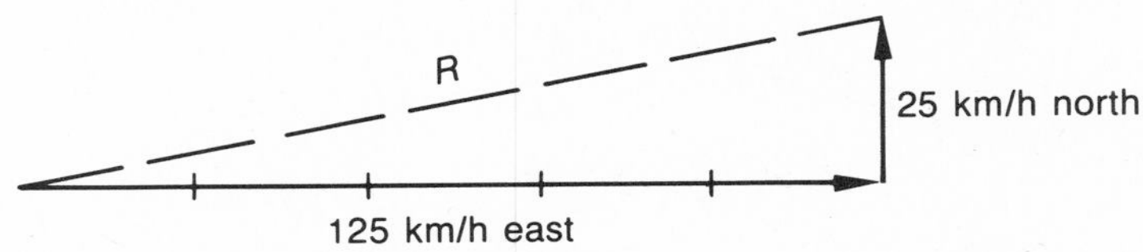

Components of Vectors

Any single vector can be thought of as a(n) _________ of two vectors, called components. Usually the components are chosen to be perpendicular, so that ____________ can be used to determine the size of each component. The diagram below shows the path of a football player running 25 m at an angle of 14° with the sideline. Complete the diagram by drawing the two component vectors, using the sideline as the component representing the player's forward progress. The magnitude of this component can be calculated using the _______ of 14°. The sideways component of the player's path can be calculated using the _______ of 14°. This process of finding components of a single vector is called ________________.

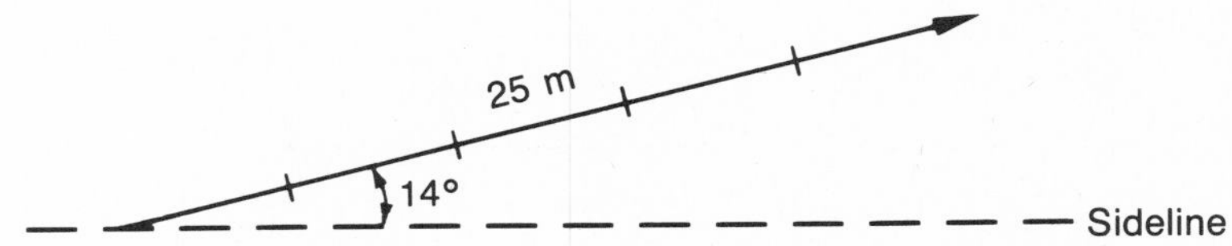

Adding Vectors at Any Angle

Vector resolution is used when adding vectors that are not ____________. Each vector is resolved into _______ components. When three vectors are added, vector resolution produces a total of _______ components. Of these components, _______ are in the horizontal direction and can be added together. The remaining _______ components are in the vertical direction and can be added together. After adding these components, there is only one _________ vector and one ________ vector. Finally, the _________ vector is found using the Pythagorean theorem.

NAME ______________________________

6.3 APPLICATIONS OF VECTORS

Equilibrium

An object is in equilibrium when the net sum, or resultant, of all forces acting on it is ______. The object will not be __________. If the sum is not zero, adding another vector will make the sum zero. The force that is represented by this added vector is called the ______________. This added force is ______ in magnitude to the resultant of the other forces, and ________ in direction to the resultant.

Gravitational Force and Inclined Planes

The weight of an object is caused by gravitational force acting on an object in a _________ direction. When an object rests on an inclined plane, this force can be resolved into ______ components that are ____________ to each other. One component is perpendicular to the surface of the inclined plane, and is equal to the force exerted by the object on the ____________. The other component is _______ to the surface of the inclined plane. This is the force that causes the object to be __________ down the inclined plane. As the inclined plane becomes steeper, this component _________ in magnitude, and acceleration _________. However, acceleration will not occur until this force overcomes friction between the ______ and the ____________. The amount of friction depends on the component force that is ____________ to the surface of the inclined plane. The amount of friction also depends on the _________________.

DATE ________ PERIOD ________ NAME ____________________

CHAPTER 7 Study Guide

Fill in the blanks as you study the chapter.

7.1 PROJECTILE MOTION

Independence of Motion in Two Dimensions

The path a projectile follows is called its ________. An object that is thrown has a(n) ________ horizontal velocity. An object that is dropped has a(n) ________ horizontal velocity that is equal to ______. In both cases, there is no horizontal force acting on the projectile after it is released, so there is no horizontal ________. Both a thrown object and a dropped object are accelerated downward by the ________. The amount of acceleration of the thrown object is ________ the amount of acceleration of the dropped object. A projectile launched from a moving source will have different trajectories when seen by observers with different ________. An observer moving with the source of the projectile will see the trajectory as having no ________ component. However, an observer not moving with the source of the projectile will see the trajectory as having both a(n) ________ and a(n) ________ component. The frame of reference affects how one sees the projectile's ________ and ________ motion, but not its ______ motion.

Objects Launched Horizontally

If a projectile is launched horizontally, its initial horizontal velocity may vary, but the initial vertical velocity is ______. The vertical acceleration is ________. The horizontal acceleration is ______. As the projectile follows its trajectory, its vertical velocity ________ while its horizontal velocity ________ ______.

Objects Launched at an Angle

If an object is bouncing, its vertical velocity is ________ as the object bounces up. Vertical velocity is ______ at the top of the path. Vertical velocity is ________ as the object falls downward. When the object returns to the launch position, the vertical speed is ________ as it was at the launch and its direction is ________. The range is the ________ distance travelled by the bouncing object. In solving projectile motion problems, the initial velocity should be resolved into its ________ and ________ components. If the launching and landing positions are at equal heights, the rising and falling times are ______. The horizontal distance moved in the first half of the trajectory is ________ the horizontal distance moved in the second half of the trajectory.

NAME ______________________________

7.2 PERIODIC MOTION

Circular Motion

If an object is moving with uniform circular motion, the speed is ________. Velocity is ________ because the direction is ________. In uniform circular motion, the radius of the path is ________. The velocity is ____________ to the radius and ________ to the circular path. Any vector that is tangent to the circle represents the __________________ at that point. All such vectors will have the same _______, but different ________. The vector that represents acceleration is in the direction of the _______, pointing toward the _______ of the circle. __________ acceleration points toward the center of the circle. It is ________ proportional to the square of the speed and ________ proportional to the radius of the circle. According to Newton's ________ law, centripetal acceleration must be caused by a(n) ______ that acts toward the center of the circle. The force that causes centripetal acceleration is called ______________. If this force disappears, the object in uniform circular motion will travel on a path that is a(n) ________ line ________ to the circle.

Changing Circular Motion: Torque

To start or stop circular motion, the force applied to the object must have a component that is ________ to the object's velocity. The product of the _______ and the _________ is called torque. The greater the torque, the ________ the change in rotational motion.

Simple Harmonic Motion

When a vibrating object is moved away from its __________ position, a force in the system pulls the object back to the __________ position. Such a force is called a(n) ____________. If this force varies linearly with the object's ____________, the motion is described as simple harmonic motion. In simple harmonic motion, the _______ is the time needed to repeat one cycle of motion. The amplitude is the maximum ____________ the object moves from the ________________. When a spring is stretched, the amount of restoring force exerted by the spring _________ linearly with the amount of force applied to the spring. This relationship is known as ____________. When a spring is stretched by the weight of an object attached to it, the period of the spring's motion depends on the ________________ and the ___________________. The period does not depend on the _________. For a pendulum, the period depends on the _______ of the pendulum. It does not depend on the _______ or the __________ of the pendulum. The _________ of a vibrating object can be increased by applying ________ forces at regular ____________, producing an effect called __________________. The time interval between the applied _______ must equal the _______ of the vibrating object.

DATE ________ PERIOD ________ NAME ____________________________

CHAPTER 8 Study Guide

Fill in the blanks as you study the chapter.

8.1 MOTION IN THE HEAVENS AND ON EARTH

Kepler's Laws of Planetary Motion

Tycho Brahe studied the motion of the planets in order to be able to ________ astronomical events. He believed that ________ was the center of the universe. Johannes Kepler believed that ________ was the center of the universe. He analyzed Brahe's data, and developed ________ laws of planetary motion. One law says that the paths of the planets are ________ with ________ located at one focus. Another law states that an imaginary line extending from the sun to a planet will sweep out equal ________ in equal amounts of time. According to this law, planets move ________ when closest to the sun and move ________ when farthest from the sun. Kepler's last law states that the ratio of the squares of the ________ of any two planets in orbit around the sun is equal to the ratio of the ________ of their distances from ________. This law can be stated as an equation, ____________. To use this law to calculate the period of a satellite, you must know the ________ of its orbit and the ________ and ________ of the orbit of another satellite.

Universal Gravitation

Newton showed that if the path of a planet were an ellipse, then the net force on the planet varies ________ with the ________ of the distance between the planet and the sun. Newton's law of universal gravitation can be stated in an equation, ____________. In this equation, F stands for ________ and ________ is the distance between the centers of the masses. G is a ________. According to this law, if the mass of one of the objects is doubled, the force of attraction is ________. If the mass of one of the objects is halved, the force of attraction is ________. If the distance between the centers of the masses is doubled, the force is decreased to ________.

Newton's Use of His Law of Universal Gravitation

Newton combined his law of universal gravitation with his ________ law of motion. Using these two laws, he was able to derive the equation for ________ third law.

Weighing Earth

The value of G was first calculated by ______________. He measured the force of ________ between two masses, and used Newton's ____________________ to calculate G. G is equal to ________________.

NAME ____________________

8.2 USING THE LAW OF UNIVERSAL GRAVITATION

Motion of Planets and Satellites

The motion of a projectile follows a(n) ________ trajectory. This path has both a(n) _______ component and a(n) _________ component. If the velocity of the _________ component is great enough, the path of the projectile will follow a curve that matches the curve of ______, and the projectile will be in ______. A satellite in an orbit that is always the same height above Earth is said to move with ___________________.

Weight and Weightlessness

The ___________ of objects due to Earth's gravitation can be calculated using the _______ square law and Newton's _______ law of motion. These calculations show that as the distance from Earth increases, the acceleration due to Earth's gravity _________. A satellite in orbit is subject to this acceleration, and it is in a condition known as _______. The downward force of gravity is unbalanced and there is no _______ force acting on a satellite in orbit. Because of the unbalanced force, the satellite and everything in it seem to be _________.

The Gravitational Field

Anything that has mass is surrounded by a ______________. The strength of this field is equal to the acceleration of _______. The strength of the field varies ________ with the _______ of the distance from the center of Earth.

Einstein's Theory of Gravity

According to Albert Einstein, gravity is not a ______, but is an effect of _______. An object that has mass causes space to be _______. When other objects move in this space, they are __________ as they move along a curve. Einstein's theory is called the general theory of ________. This theory explains why the path of light can be deflected when it passes the ______. This theory also explains that no light escapes from a(n) _________ because the light is completely turned around by the huge amount of ______.

DATE ________ PERIOD ________ NAME ______________________________

CHAPTER 9 Study Guide

Fill in the blanks as you study the chapter.

9.1 IMPULSE AND CHANGE IN MOMENTUM

Momentum and Impulse

The amount of force needed to change the motion of a moving object depends on the ________ and ______ of the object. The momentum of a body is the product of the body's ______ and ________. Momentum is a(n) _______ quantity. Its direction is ___________ the direction of the velocity. The equation used to calculate momentum is ________. In this equation, *p* stands for ___________, *m* stands for ______, and *v* stands for ________. The unit for momentum is the ____________________. The product of the ______ applied to an object and the ___________ over which it acts is called the impulse. The direction of the impulse is ___________ the direction of the force that is applied. The unit for impulse is the ______________. The impulse given to an object is equal to the change in the object's ___________. This equality is the ________________ theorem. It is also another statement of Newton's ________ law of motion.

Angular Momentum

If a(n) _______ is applied to an object moving in a circle, the speed of the object changes. The quantity of angular motion that is similar to linear ___________ is called angular momentum. To calculate the angular momentum of a body, the body's ______, ________, and ________ from the center of rotation must be known. The angular momentum of a planet in orbit is ________, although the distance from the sun varies. The planet's ________ also varies, and is greatest when the planet is __________ the sun.

NAME ______________________________

9.2 THE CONSERVATION OF MOMENTUM

Newton's Third Law and Momentum

If one object collides with another, the momentum of each object ________. The first object exerts a(n) ______ on the second object, and the second object exerts a(n) ______ of ______ magnitude and ________ direction on the first object. If objects neither leave nor enter a system, the system is described as _______. If no external forces act on a system, the system is described as ________. When there is a collision within such a system, the net change in momentum is ______. The total momentum before the collision is ________ the total momentum after the collision.

Law of Conservation of Momentum

In a closed, isolated system, the momentum ________________. This statement is the law of ________________________. When two objects within the system collide, the magnitude of the momentum lost by one of the objects is ________ the momentum gained by the other object. Momentum can be __________ from one object in the _______ to another.

Internal and External Forces

Internal forces act between objects in _________ system. External forces are exerted by objects ________ the system. The total momentum of a system is conserved only when there are no ________ forces acting on the system.

Conservation of Momentum in Two Dimensions

The law of conservation of momentum does not depend on the _________ in which objects move before and after colliding. The momentum of two objects in a system can be represented by two ________, which can be resolved into vertical and horizontal ___________. After all vectors are added, the final sum must equal the _______ momentum of the system.

DATE ________ PERIOD ________ NAME ____________________________

CHAPTER 10 Study Guide

Fill in the blanks as you study the chapter.

10.1 WORK AND ENERGY

Work

Work is the product of the ______ exerted on an object and the ________ the object moves in the ________ of the force. The equation used to calculate work is ________. In this equation, *W* stands for ______, *F* stands for ______, and *d* stands for ________. Work has no direction, so it is a ______ quantity. The SI unit of work is the ______. When a force of one _______ moves an object a distance of one ______, one ______ of work is done. Work is done on an object only if the object ______. Work is done only if the ______ and the ____________ are in the same direction.

Work and Direction of Force

If a force is exerted ______________ the motion, work is done. If a force is exerted ____________ to the motion, no work is done. If a force is exerted at another angle to the motion, only the component of the force ______________ the motion does work. The magnitude of this component is found by multiplying the force applied by the _______ of the angle between the force and the ______________. When friction opposes motion, the work done by friction is ________. When work is done on an object, _______ is transferred. Work is the transfer of _______ as the result of _______. This transfer can be _______ or ________.

Power

Power is the ______ of doing work, or the ______ at which _______ is transferred. The equation used to calculate power is _______. In this equation, *P* stands for _______, *W* stands for ______, and *t* stands for ______. The unit of power is the ______. One ______ of energy transferred in ___________ equals one watt. This is a very small unit, so power is often measured in ________.

CHAPTER 10 Study Guide

NAME ______________________________

10.2 MACHINES

Simple and Complex Machines

A machine eases the load by changing the __________ or ________ of a force. A machine does not change the amount of _______ that is done. When a machine is used, the work that is done to the machine is called the __________. The work that the machine does is the __________. The machine ________ energy, but is not a _______ of energy. The machine's _______ work cannot be larger than the _______ work.

Energy Conservation and Mechanical Advantage

The force that is exerted _______ a machine is the effort force. The force exerted _______ a machine is the resistance force. The _______ of these forces is the mechanical advantage of the machine. The equation used to calculate mechanical advantage is __________. When the mechanical advantage is greater than one, the machine __________ the force that is applied. If a machine transfers all of the energy, the output work _______ the input work. The distances moved can be used to calculate the ________________________, using the equation ____________. The efficiency of a machine is the ______ of the output work to the input work. An ideal machine has an efficiency of _______. A real machine has an efficiency of ______________. The lower the efficiency, the ________ the effort force needed to produce the same __________ force. The lever, pulley, and inclined planes are examples of ______________.

Compound Machines

A compound machine is made up of ___________ simple machines, which are linked so that the __________ force of one machine becomes the ______ force of the next machine. The mechanical advantage of a compound machine is the ________ of the mechanical advantages of the simple machines of which it is made.

The Human Walking Machine

Many body structures are _______, which are simple machines. In these human systems, a bone forms a(n) ________ and muscle contractions are a source of _______. The movable joints between bones form a(n) ________. The __________ is the weight of the body or any object being moved by the body. The mechanical advantages of these systems are ______, and use a large amount of ________.

DATE __________ PERIOD ________ NAME ____

CHAPTER 11 Study Guide

Fill in the blanks as you study the chapter.

11.1 ENERGY IN ITS MANY FORMS

Forms of Energy

A moving object is able to change ______ and its ____________. Moving objects have ________ energy. This energy comes from stored energy that is called _________ energy. Energy is transferred to an object when _______ is done on the object. The amount of potential energy an object has depends on the object's ________, _______, or ______.

Doing Work to Change Kinetic Energy

An object's kinetic energy is proportional to the ______ of the object. Kinetic energy is also proportional to the square of the ________. The equation used to calculate kinetic energy is ___________. The unit used to measure kinetic energy is the ______. Increasing the amount of work done on an object __________ the amount of kinetic energy the object receives. According to the work-energy theorem, the _________ done on an object is equal to its ________ in kinetic and potential energy. The net work done on an object is positive if the net force acts in the _______ direction as the motion. If net work is positive, the object's kinetic energy __________. The net work done is negative if the net force acts in the _________ direction to the motion. If the net work is negative, the object's kinetic energy __________.

Potential Energy

In a moving object, kinetic energy can be changed to _________ energy and then to ________ energy. The total energy of the object is the sum of its _______________ and _____________. When a ball is thrown in the air, all of its energy is _______ energy at the start of its flight. This energy is changed into _________ energy. When the ball reaches its highest point, its speed is ______. At this point, it has no _______ energy, only _________ energy. As the ball falls downward, its speed __________ and _________ energy is changed to _______ energy. The equation used to calculate potential energy is ___________. In this equation, h stands for _______, which is measured against another position, called the __________ _______. This formula is only valid if acceleration is _________.

CHAPTER 11 Study Guide

NAME ______________________________

11.2 CONSERVATION OF ENERGY

Systems

In a closed, isolated system, objects do not ______ or ______, and no ________ forces act on the system. Under these conditions, the law of ____________________ states that energy can change ______, but the total amount of energy is ________. According to this law, energy cannot be ________ or ________. In a closed, isolated system, the sum of the potential and kinetic energy of an object can be called the __________ energy. If there is an increase in an object's kinetic energy, there will be a(n) _________ in its potential energy. The ______________ motion of a pendulum can show the law of conservation of energy. When the pendulum bob is raised to start the motion, it is given ________ energy. As the bob moves downward, the amount of _______ energy increases. At the lowest point of the pendulum bob's swing, it has zero ________ energy, and the maximum amount of _______ energy. As the pendulum bob swings upward, the potential energy _________ and the kinetic energy _________. The pendulum eventually stops swinging because of _______ between the pendulum and the ______. The pendulum's energy is changed into another form, _____________, and the pendulum bob would be ________ to the touch. According to Albert Einstein, ______ is another form of potential energy, called its ______ energy. If an object is distorted, the energy that is used to distort the object increases the object's ______ slightly.

Analyzing Collisions

When two objects collide, their ________ change slightly. In this change, kinetic energy is changed into _________ energy. After the collision, the energy is changed back into _______ energy. If ______ of the kinetic energy that was present before the collision is changed into kinetic energy again, the collision is said to be elastic. In this collision, momentum is __________. If ______ of the kinetic energy that was present before the collision is changed into kinetic energy again, the collision is said to be inelastic. Some of the energy is changed into __________. In an inelastic collision, momentum is __________.

DATE ________ PERIOD ________ NAME ________________________

CHAPTER 12 Study Guide

Fill in the blanks as you study the chapter.

12.1 TEMPERATURE AND THERMAL ENERGY

What Makes a Hot Body Hot?

Matter is made up of tiny ________ that are constantly ________. The particles in an object that is ______ move faster than the particles in an object that is ______. The idea that particles in an object are in motion is the ______________ theory. The particles in a solid are held together by ______________ forces. Because the particles are vibrating, they have _______ energy. However, the particles also have ________ energy. The ______ of these two amounts of energy makes up the internal, or ________, energy of the object.

Thermal Energy and Temperature

An object that is ______ has more thermal energy than a similar object that is ______. The particles in a hot object have ______ kinetic and potential _______ than the particles in a cold object. Because particles show a range of energies, it is the ________ energy of particles that is higher in a(n) ______ object than in a(n) ______ one. The temperature of a(n) ______ is proportional to the average _______ energy of the particles. The temperature of a(n) ______ or a(n) ______ is approximately proportional to the average _______ energy of the particles. Temperature does not depend on the ________ of particles in the object. Thermal energy does depend on the ________ of particles in the object.

Equilibrium and Thermometry

When a glass thermometer is placed into a hot liquid, the particles in the ______ hit the particles in the ______, transferring ________. As the particles in the glass of the thermometer gain energy, they begin to transfer energy to the ______, and the liquid and thermometer are in thermal ___________. At this time, the thermometer and the liquid are at the same ___________, although they may have different amounts of ______________. A thermometer depends on a ________ that changes with temperature. In an alcohol thermometer, the ________ of the alcohol increases with temperature. In a liquid crystal thermometer, the ______ of the crystals changes with temperature. Each kind of crystal in the thermometer changes ______ at a different ___________.

CHAPTER 12 Study Guide

NAME ______________________________

Temperature Scales: Celsius and Kelvin

Anders Celsius based a temperature scale on the properties of ______. On the Celsius scale, the ________ point of water is 0°C, and the ________ point of water is 100°C. Temperatures do not seem to have a(n) _______ limit, but they do have a(n) ______ limit. This limit is called ____________, and is the basis of the _______ scale. On this scale, the symbol K stands for the _______, which is equal to one ________ degree. The freezing point of ______ is 273.15 K. The boiling point of water is ________.

Heat and Thermal Energy

When a body is placed in contact with a hotter body, the temperature of the cooler body __________, because ________ flows from the hotter body to the cooler one. Heat is the ________ that flows as a result of a difference in ____________. Heat is represented by the symbol ______, and is measured in _______. ______________ is the energy that an object contains, but ______ is the energy that is transferred between objects. When heat flows into an object, the object's _____________ and ___________ increase. The amount of increase depends on the _______ and specific heat of the object. The specific heat of a material is the amount of ________ that must be added to _______ the temperature of a unit mass ______ temperature unit. Specific heat is represented by the symbol _______, and is measured in _______. Compared to most other materials, the specific heat of water is _______. The heat gained or lost by an object as its temperature changes can be calculated using the equation ___________. In this equation, _______ is the amount of heat lost or gained, _______ is the mass of the object, _______ is the specific heat of the substance, and _______ is the change in temperature.

Calorimetry: Measuring Specific Heat

A calorimeter is used to measure changes in ______________. A measured ______ of a substance is heated to a known ____________, and added to a known mass of ______ at a known temperature in a calorimeter. The temperature of the _______ increases. The change in thermal energy is calculated from the temperature change of the ______. The calorimeter is insulated so that ________ will be conserved in a closed, isolated ________. Because the heated object loses thermal energy, its energy change is ________. Because the water gains energy, its energy change is ________.

NAME ____________________

12.2 CHANGE OF STATE AND LAWS OF THERMODYNAMICS

Change of State

If the temperature of a solid is raised, it changes to a(n) ______ and then to a(n) ______. This occurs because a(n) ________ in thermal energy of a solid increases the _______ and _________ energies of the particles. As the solid is heated, its particles cannot be held in place by the _______ among them. When the particles are moving freely enough to slide past each other, the substance has changed from a(n) ______ to a(n) ______. The ___________ at which this change occurs is the melting point of the substance. During the melting process, the ________ energy of the particles increases, but the temperature _______________. The amount of energy needed to ______ one ______ of a substance is called the heat of fusion of the substance. For an object at its melting point, adding this energy changes the object's ______, but not its ___________. If the substance is heated after melting is complete, the temperature _________. When the temperature reaches the ___________, another change of state takes place. During this change of state the temperature ______________. The amount of _______ needed to vaporize one ______ of a liquid is called the heat of ___________. The amount of heat needed to melt a solid is calculated using the equation _________. In this equation, ______ stands for heat, ______ stands for the mass of the solid, and ______ stands for the heat of fusion. The amount of heat needed to vaporize a liquid is calculated using the equation _________. In this equation, H_v stands for ________________. To melt a solid or vaporize a liquid, heat must be ______. To condense a gas or freeze a liquid, heat must be ________.

The First Law of Thermodynamics

The thermal energy of an object can be increased if ______ is transferred to it or if ______ is done on it, changing __________ energy into ________ energy. Other forms of energy that can be converted into thermal energy include ______, ______, and _________ energy. The first law of thermodynamics states that the total ________ in the thermal energy of a system is the ______ of the work done on it and the heat added to it. The first law of thermodynamics is another way of stating the law of __________________. A device that converts ________ energy to ___________ energy continuously is called a heat engine. Heat engines require a ______ temperature _______ from which thermal energy can be removed, and a ______ temperature ______ into which thermal energy can be delivered. In an automobile engine, a mixture of ______ and _________ is ignited, producing a high temperature ______. The air in the cylinder is heated and it ________, pushing on a(n) _______. This push changes ________ energy into ___________ energy. Some of the thermal energy does not get converted, but instead heats the _____________ and ____________. This thermal energy is transferred out of the engine and is called ___________. The heat from the flame is equal to the sum of the ________________ produced by the engine and the ___________ expelled from the engine. A refrigerator is a device that

NAME ____

removes thermal energy from a ________ body and transfers it to a ________ body. An external source of ________ is needed to cause the transfer. A fluid, such as ________ is used to transfer ________ from the food in the refrigerator to the air in the room. A heat pump is a ____________ that can be run in two directions. In summer, heat is transferred from the house to the ____________. In the winter, heat is transferred from the ____________ to the house. Both transfers require the use of ____________ energy.

The Second Law of Thermodynamics

Sadi Carnot proved that all engines produce ____________. This is because all systems contain some disorder, or ________. When heat energy is added to a system, particles move in a ________ way. The increase in motion of particles ___________ the entropy of the system. The second law of _________________ states that natural processes go in a direction that __________ the total entropy of the universe. When two objects of different temperatures are brought together, they reach thermal ____________, and their temperatures are the same. The entropy of the system at its final temperature is ________ than the entropy of the system before reaching the final temperature. Entropy is often used as a measure of the ______________ of energy. Because the waste heat from an engine or a furnace cannot be used to do ______, the energy is not considered to be _________.

DATE ________ PERIOD ________ NAME ______________________________

CHAPTER 13 Study Guide

Fill in the blanks as you study the chapter.

13.1 THE FLUID STATE

Pressure

A fluid is any material that ______ and offers little resistance to a change in its shape when under ________. Fluids include _______ and _______. According to the _______________ theory, gases are made up of ________ that are in constant ________ motion, and make _______ collisions with one another and with their container. The pressure that a gas exerts on its container is the result of ________ between gas particles and the walls of the container. Pressure is the ______ exerted on a unit ______. Pressure can be calculated using the equation ________. In this equation, *p* stands for ________, *A* stands for ______, and *F* stands for ______. The SI unit of pressure is the ______ which is represented by the symbol ______. A force of one ________ acting over one ____________ produces a pressure of one pascal. One __________ is equal to 1000 Pa.

Fluids at Rest—Hydrostatics

In an ideal fluid, there is no _______ among the particles of the fluid. Blaise Pascal noted that the _______ of a container does not affect the pressure at any given _______. According to Pascal's principle, any change in _________ applied to a fluid in a container is ___________ throughout the fluid. Pascal's principle is the basis for _________ systems, in which a fluid is used to ________ a force. The fluid in a hydraulic system is in two chambers, each of which contains a movable _______. The force that is transmitted through the system can be calculated by using the equation __________. In this equation, ______ and ______ represent the two forces; ______ and ______ represent the areas of the two pistons. Pressure is proportional to the ______ and _______ of the fluid. For an object immersed in a fluid, there is a net force in a(n) _______ direction exerted by the fluid. This force is called the ________ force. The volume of the immersed object is equal to the ________ of the fluid that is displaced. The buoyant force is equal to the _______ of the fluid that is displaced. This relationship is known as ___________________. The buoyant force depends only on the weight of the ______________, not the weight of the _______. If the density of an object is greater than the density of the fluid in which it is placed, the object will ______. If the density of the object is less than the density of the fluid in which it is placed, the object will ______.

Fluids in Motion—Hydrodynamics

The relationship between the ________ of a fluid and the _________ exerted by the fluid is described by __________ principle. Airfoils are devices that use this principle to produce ______ when moving through a(n) ______. An airplane wing is curved so that the ______ surface has a greater curve than the

CHAPTER 13 Study Guide

NAME ______________________________

________ surface. Air moving over the top of the wing moves a(n) ________ distance, and therefore travels at a(n) ________ speed. The air pressure over the wing is ________ the pressure under the wing. There is a net force in a(n) ________ direction. This force is called ________. The ________ of a fluid can be represented by streamlines. The closer the streamlines are to each other, the greater the ________ and the lower the ________ of the fluid. Streamlines that swirl indicate that the fluid is ________, and that ________________ does not apply to the situation.

Liquids vs Gases

Unlike a gas, a liquid has a(n) ________ volume. A gas is ________ compressible than a liquid. The particles in a liquid are ______________ than the particles in a gas. The particles in a liquid exert ______________ forces of attraction called ________ forces.

Surface Tension

The ________ forces among the particles in a liquid cause the surface of a liquid to have the ________ possible area. This tendency causes the phenomenon known as the ______________ of a liquid. Within a liquid, there is no ________ acting on the particles. At the surface there is a net force acting in a(n) __________ direction, causing the surface layer of particles to be ____________. Liquids form spherical drops because the sphere is the shape that has the ______ surface for a given volume. Adhesion is an attractive force between particles of ________ substances. Adhesion causes capillary action, which is the ______ of water inside a narrow ______.

Evaporation and Condensation

In a liquid, the particles move at ________ speeds. Only a particle that is near the ________ and moving ______ can escape from the liquid. This escape is called ____________. As particles escape, the remaining liquid becomes ______, because the average ____________ of the remaining particles is decreased. A volatile liquid evaporates ______ than a liquid that is not volatile. If a water molecule in the air strikes a cool surface, the molecule may lose ____________ and remain on the cool surface. The water is said to have __________ on the surface. Fog forms when water vapor in the air __________ on particles of ______ in the air.

Plasma

If the temperature of a gas is increased enough, the ________ between the particles become violent and ________ are pulled off the atoms. The state of matter that is produced is called ________, and contains positively-charged ______ and negatively-charged ________. The main difference between a gas and a plasma is that only the ________ can conduct electricity.

CHAPTER 13 Study Guide

NAME ______________________________

13.2 THE SOLID STATE

Solid Bodies

When the temperature of a liquid is lowered, the average kinetic energy of particles __________. The particles move _______, and become _______ into a fixed pattern. In a crystal lattice, the only motion of particles is ________ around fixed positions. In an amorphous solid, the particles are in _______ positions, but a(n) ________ pattern. An amorphous solid can be classified as a viscous _______. For most substances, the solid state is _______ dense than the liquid state. However, water is an exception to this rule, reaching its greatest density at a temperature of _______. For most liquids, the freezing point __________ as the pressure on the liquid increases. _______ is an exception to this rule.

Elasticity of Solids

A(n) ________ force may cause an object to twist or bend out of shape. Elasticity is the ability of an object to _______ to its original shape after the external force is _________. If the object does not return to its original form, its ___________ has been reached. Elasticity depends on ______________ forces. Malleability is the ability to be rolled into a _______. Ductility is the ability to be drawn into a _______.

Thermal Expansion of Matter

Most materials ________ when heated and ________ when cooled, a property known as ________________. This property causes ___________ currents in fluids. When a solid is heated, its particles vibrate ______ violently, which __________ the forces of attraction between particles and __________ the separation between particles. The change in length of a solid is proportional to its change in ____________ and to its _______. The change in _______ can be calculated using the equation $\Delta L = \alpha L_1 \Delta T$. In this equation, _______ stands for the change in length, _______ stands for the initial length, and _______ stands for the change in temperature. The symbol α stands for the ___________________________. The __________ strips used in thermostat switches make use of thermal expansion. The side of the strip that expands more is on the ________ of the curve when the strip is heated, and on the _______ of the curve when the strip is cooled.

DATE ________ PERIOD ________ NAME ________________________

CHAPTER 14 Study Guide

Fill in the blanks as you study the chapter.

14.1 WAVE PROPERTIES

Types of Waves

Water waves and sound waves are ____________ waves. These waves require a(n) _________ medium. Light waves and radio waves are _______________ waves. These waves require _______ medium. Electrons and other _________ show wave-like properties, called _______ waves. There are ______ kinds of mechanical waves. In a transverse wave, particles of the medium vibrate _____________ to the direction of the ________ of the wave. In a longitudinal wave, particles of the medium vibrate ________ to the direction of the ________ of the wave. ________ waves are a mixture of transverse and longitudinal waves. In these waves, particles of the medium vibrate ________ and _____________ to the direction of the wave. A wave pulse is a(n) _______ disturbance that travels through a medium. A traveling wave is a(n) ___________ wave produced by a source that is _________ with simple __________ motion.

The Measures of a Wave: Frequency, Wavelength, and Velocity

The period of a wave is the _________ time interval in which the ________ repeats itself. The frequency of a wave is the number of complete __________ per ________ measured at a fixed location. Frequency is measured in units called ______, which are represented by ______. One vibration per second is equal to one ______. The frequency and period of a wave are related in the equation ________. In this equation, ______ stands for time and ______ stands for frequency. The shortest distance between points where the wave pattern repeats itself is the ___________ of the wave, and is represented by the Greek letter ______. The ______ points of each wave are called crests, and the ______ points are called troughs. The velocity of a wave can be calculated by using the equation ________.

Amplitude of a Wave

The __________ displacement from the rest, or __________, position is the amplitude of a wave. It takes ______ work to produce a wave with a large amplitude than it does to produce a wave with a small amplitude. The larger the amplitude of the wave, the more ________ is transferred.

CHAPTER 14 Study Guide

NAME ____________________

14.2 WAVE INTERFERENCE

Waves at Boundaries Between Media

The speed of a mechanical wave does not depend on the __________ or the __________ of the wave. It only depends on the __________ of the medium. In a given medium, the speed of a wave with a large amplitude is ________ the speed of a wave with a small amplitude. In a given medium, the speed of a high-frequency wave is ________ the speed of a low-frequency wave. When a wave reaches a boundary between one medium and another, the wave that reaches the boundary is called the ________ wave. The wave that moves through the new medium is called the ___________ wave. Some of the ________ of the incident wave moves backward from the boundary and is called the ________ wave. If the difference between the two media is small, _______ of the energy of the incident wave will be transmitted. If the difference between the two media is great, ______ of the energy will be transmitted. When a wave passes from a less dense to a more dense medium, the reflected wave is ________. When a wave passes from a more dense to a less dense medium, the reflected wave is _______. When a wave is transmitted from one medium to another, the __________ of the wave does not change. The _______ and the ___________ of the wave do change.

Superposition of Waves

When two or more waves move through a medium, each wave affects the medium _____________. According to the principle of superposition, the _____________ of a medium caused by two or more waves is the algebraic _______ of the _____________ caused by the individual waves. Interference is the result of the _____________ of two or more waves. Constructive interference occurs when the wave displacements are in __________ direction, and results in a wave with a(n) ________ displacement. After the two pulses have passed each other, they have their original _______ and ______. Destructive interference occurs when the wave displacements are in _________ directions. If the amplitudes of the two pulses are equal but opposite, the displacement produced when the pulses meet is _______. If the amplitudes are unequal, _____________________ will not be complete.

Standing Waves

When two waves meet, a point in the medium that is always ____________ by the wave is called a node. A node is produced by ___________ interference. When two waves meet, the point in the medium where there is the greatest _____________ is called an antinode. An antinode is produced by ____________ interference. If the period of a wave is equal to the time it takes for the wave to travel to a fixed point and back, a(n) _________ wave is produced. In this wave, the nodes and antinodes are __________ and the wave appears to be ____________.

CHAPTER 14 Study Guide

NAME ________________________________

Reflection of Waves

The direction of waves moving in two or three dimensions is shown by ______ diagrams. The ray that reaches a barrier is called the ________ ray. The ray that moves back from the barrier is called the ________ ray. The direction of the barrier is shown by a line drawn at a(n) __________ to the barrier. This line is called the ________. The angle between the ________ ray and the ________ is called the angle of incidence. The angle between the ________ ray and the ________ is called the angle of reflection. The law of _________ states that the angle of incidence equals the angle of reflection.

Refraction of Waves

In water waves, the velocity is _______ in shallower water. If the incident ray is parallel to the normal, there is a change in the velocity and ___________ of the wave. If the incident ray is not parallel to the normal, there is a change in velocity, wavelength, and ________ of the wave. The change in ________ of a wave at the boundary between two media is called refraction.

Diffraction and Interference of Waves

When waves reach a small opening in a barrier, they form ________ waves that spread out from the opening. This spreading of waves is called __________. The smaller the ___________ in comparison to the size of the barrier, the ______ the diffraction. When there are two openings in a barrier, ______ sets of circular waves are produced. When the new waves interfere with each other, ___________ interference produces large waves, and __________ interference produces a line of nodes.

DATE ________ PERIOD ________ NAME ________________________

CHAPTER 15 Study Guide

Fill in the blanks as you study the chapter.

15.1 PROPERTIES OF SOUND

Sound Waves

Sound waves are __________ waves, produced by the __________ and __________ of matter. In air, sound waves are produced when a vibrating ________ causes regular variations in __________. The ________ of a sound wave is the number of oscillations in __________ each second. The ________ of sound in air depends on air temperature. In solids and liquids, the velocity of air is __________ it is in gases. Sounds cannot travel through a(n) ________. Sound waves can be ________ by a hard surface, causing a(n) ______. The reflection of sound waves can be used to find the ________ between a source and a reflector. Ships that are equipped with ______ make use of sound reflection. Sound waves can be ________ when they pass through a narrow opening. Sound waves can ________ and produce nodes where little sound is heard. The __________ is the distance between adjacent regions of maximum ________. The equation that relates velocity, frequency, and wavelength is ________.

The Doppler Shift

The Doppler shift causes sounds to seem _______ in frequency when the source is moving toward the listener, and ______ in frequency when the source is moving away from the listener. The ________ of the source of the sound does not change. The Doppler shift is used in the ______ that measures the speed of automobiles. It is also used in astronomy to measure the ______ of galaxies and infer the ________ to them.

Pitch and Loudness

The ________ of a sound wave is heard as pitch. The ________ of a sound wave is heard as loudness. The notes of the musical scale have different __________. Notes with frequencies that give ratios of small ______ numbers sound pleasing when heard together. Notes in a ratio of 2:1 are said to be a(n) ______ apart. Sound levels are measured in ________ and indicate sound ________. Sound level is a ratio of the ____________ of a given sound wave to the ____________ of the most ______ heard sound level.

CHAPTER 15 Study Guide

NAME ______________________________

15.2 THE SOUND OF MUSIC

Sources of Sound

Sound is produced by a(n) ________ object. The human voice is produced when the __________ vibrate. The frequency of the vibration is controlled by the ________ that put tension on the vocal cords. In a trumpet, the __________ vibrate. In a clarinet, the ______ vibrates. In a flute, a column of ______ vibrates. In a guitar, the _______ vibrate.

Resonance

In a trumpet or clarinet, sound is heard only when the ______ in the tube of the instrument vibrates at the same _________ as the lips or reed. This effect is called _________. The pitch of the instrument is changed by changing the ______ of the column of vibrating ______. A closed pipe is a resonating tube with ________ closed. When sound waves reflected through the pipe reinforce each other, a(n) ________ wave is produced. There is a pressure ________ at the point of reflection, and a pressure ______ at the open end of the tube. The shortest closed pipe that can produce a standing wave is __________________ long. An open pipe resonator has both ends ______. There is a pressure ______ at each end, and at least one pressure ________ between. The shortest open pipe that can produce a standing wave is ________________ long.

Detection of Sound

Sound detectors convert the _______ energy of air molecules into ______________ energy. The ______ is the sound detector of the human body. It consists of three parts: the __________, __________, and _________. The ______ ear collects sound. The sound causes the ________ to vibrate. Then three ______ in the _______ ear vibrate. The vibrations are transmitted to the oval window in the ______ ear. In the ________, fluid vibrates, which causes tiny hair cells to vibrate and stimulate __________. The sensation is interpreted by the ______. Older people are ______ sensitive to high frequencies than are young people. Exposure to ___________ can cause the ear to lose sensitivity to sounds because of damage to the _________ in the inner ear.

The Quality of Sound

Most sounds are made up of several __________. The quality of the sound depends on the relative _________ of the frequencies. Sound quality is called _______. If two waves of slightly different frequencies reach the ear, the ______ of the two waves has a(n) _________ that oscillates in intensity. The listener hears a pulsing variation in ________, called a(n) _____. The frequency of the ______ is the _________ in the frequencies of the two waves. If there are more beats than the ear can distinguish, the ear detects a ________ wave. If the sound is __________, it is called a dissonance. If the sound is ________, it is called a consonance, or a(n) ______. Musical instruments

CHAPTER 15 Study Guide

NAME ____

that have _____ resonators produce sounds that have more than one _________ frequency. The lowest of these frequencies is called the ___________, and whole-number multiples of the lowest frequency are called __________. An open-pipe resonator produces the fundamental and ______ harmonics. A closed-pipe resonator produces the fundamental and ______ harmonics. Sound distortion occurs when sounds of different ___________ are transmitted with different efficiencies. Noise consists of many different ___________ with ______ relationship. If all frequencies have equal _________, the result is called white noise. The resonator of the human voice is the ______ and ____________. The _______ of the resonator is changed by the movements of the tongue and teeth, and changes the ________ of harmonics present.

DATE ________ PERIOD ________ NAME ____________________________

CHAPTER 16 Study Guide

Fill in the blanks as you study the chapter.

16.1 LIGHT FUNDAMENTALS

The Facts of Light

Light is the range of ________ of ________ waves that stimulates the retina of the eye. The shortest wavelengths of light are about ________ long and are ______ in color. The longest wavelengths of light are about ________ long, and are ______ in color. In a vacuum or ________ medium, light travels in a(n) ________ line. This description of the path of light is the ______ model. A ray is a straight line that represents the path of a very narrow ______ of light. Ray optics is the use of ray ________ to study light and describe how it is ________ and refracted.

The Speed of Light

________ was the first person to hypothesize that light has a finite speed, although he was unable to measure it. The first measurement of the speed of light was made by ________, who made measurements based on one of the moons of ________. The speed of light is the product of its ________ and ________. The equation that shows this relationship is ______. The symbol used to represent the speed of light is ______. The International Committee on Weights and Measures has defined the speed of light in a vacuum to be exactly ______________. Expressed to three significant figures, the speed of light is ______________.

Sources of Light

A body that ______ light waves is said to be luminous and a body that ________ light waves is said to be illuminated. An incandescent object is a(n) ________ body that gives off light as a result of being ______. The ______ at which light is emitted by a source is luminous flux, which is represented by ______, and is expressed in a unit called the ______. The illumination of a surface is called the ________, which is measured in lumens per square meter, or ______. If the distance from a surface to a point source of light is doubled, the illumination reaching the surface is ________ as great. The candela is a measure of luminous ________. Luminous intensity is equal to luminous ______ divided by ______. To increase the illumination on a surface, ________ the luminous flux of the light source or ________ the distance between the source and the surface. The equation used to determine illuminance is ________. In this equation, *E* represents ________, *P* represents the ________ of the source, and ______ represents the distance from the surface. This equation is only valid if a line that points to the bulb is ________ to the source and if the source can be considered to be a ______ source.

CHAPTER 16 Study Guide

NAME ____________________

16.2 LIGHT AND MATTER

Color

Materials that transmit light waves are described as __________. Materials that transmit light waves, but do not permit objects to be seen clearly, are described as __________. Materials that are described as opaque ________ or _______ the light waves that fall on them. The arrangement of colors from _______ to _______ is called the spectrum, and was named by ________, who showed that _______ light is made up of colors. Each color is associated with a specific __________. In the ________ color process, adding together red, green, and blue light produces _________. These three colors are called the ________ colors of light. When _______ of the primary colors are mixed, a secondary color of light is formed. These three colors are ________, _______, and _________. For each primary color there is a(n) __________ color that is its complementary color. Complementary colors add to form __________. The complementary color of red is _______. Dyes and pigments ________ certain wavelengths and ________ or _______ other wavelengths. If all wavelengths are _________, no light is reflected and an object appears _______. The absorption of light forms colors by the __________ process. A(n) ________ pigment absorbs one color. A(n) _________ pigment absorbs two colors. Yellow and cyan are two of the ________ pigments. Red and blue are two of the __________ pigments. When complementary pigments are combined, the result is _______.

Formation of Colors in Thin Films

The colors seen in a soap bubble are caused by constructive and destructive __________ of light waves. This occurs because the _________ of a soap film varies. Some light is _________ by the surface of the film and some light is __________. The transmitted light is ________ by the back surface of the film. The reflected waves of some wavelengths ________ each other, while the waves of other wavelengths ________ with each other. As a result, each color of light is _________ by a different area of the film.

Polarization of Light

Only _________ waves can be polarized. The waves in a beam of light vibrate in every direction ___________ to the direction of travel. A polarizing filter allows the waves vibrating in _________ to pass through, and the light is said to be ________. If the plane of a second polarizing filter is ___________ to the plane of the first, no light passes through the second filter. If the plane of the second filter is _______ to the plane of the first, most of the light will be transmitted.

DATE ________ PERIOD ________ NAME ____________________

CHAPTER 17 Study Guide

Fill in the blanks as you study the chapter.

17.1 HOW LIGHT BEHAVES AT A BOUNDARY

The Law of Reflection

When a light ray strikes a reflecting surface, the angle of reflection is ________ the angle of incidence. Both angles are measured from a(n) ________, which is ____________ to the reflecting surface. When a beam of light strikes a rough surface, it reflects in ______ directions, producing a(n) ______ reflection. When a beam of light strikes a smooth surface, the reflected rays are __________ each other, producing a(n) ________ reflection.

Refraction of Light

The ________ of light at the __________ between two media is called refraction. The angle of incidence is measured between the ___________ and the ________. The angle of refraction is measured between the ___________ and the ________. Refraction does not occur if the angle of incidence is ______. When this happens, the ray changes ______ but it does not change direction. As a light ray enters a more optically dense medium, its speed __________, and the refracted ray bends ________ the normal. As a light ray passes into a medium in which it travels faster, the refracted ray bends __________ the normal.

Snell's Law

Snell's law states that a ray of light bends in such a way that the ______ of the ______ of the angle of incidence to the ______ of the angle of refraction is a constant. This constant is called the ________________ if the light is moving from a(n) ________ to another medium. For a ray traveling from one medium into another, Snell's law is written as the equation, ______________. In the equation, ______ is the index of refraction of the incident medium and ______ is the index of refraction of the second medium. The angle of incidence is represented by ______ and the angle of refraction is represented by ______.

Index of Refraction and the Speed of Light

The speed of light depends on the ________ in which it travels. The index of refraction is a measure of the amount that light ______ when passing into the medium from a(n) ________. The index of refraction can be calculated by comparing the ______ of light in a vacuum to the ______ of light in the medium. The equation for this is __________.

CHAPTER 17 Study Guide

NAME ________________________________

17.2 APPLICATIONS OF REFLECTED AND REFRACTED LIGHT

Total Internal Reflection

Total internal reflection occurs when light passes from a(n) ______ optically dense medium to a(n) ______ optically dense medium at an angle so great that there is no ________ ray. The critical angle is the ________ angle that causes the refracted ray to lie along the _________ of the substance. If the angle of incidence is greater than the critical angle, the incident ray cannot be ________, but instead is ________. Light is internally reflected in optical fibers because the main glass fiber is coated with a glass that has a(n) ______ index of refraction.

Effects of Refraction

A mirage of a puddle is seen on a road if the road is very ______. The road heats the air above it, which changes the ________________ of the air. A ray of light aimed toward the road is bent __________ the normal, and more ________ to the road. An object submerged in a liquid may appear to be ______ ______ the surface of the liquid than it really is. Light is refracted by the atmosphere so that sunlight is visible _______ sunrise and ______ sunset.

Dispersion of Light

The index of refraction depends on the __________ of the incident light. In most materials, red light travels _______ and has the ________ index of refraction. Violet light travels ________ and has the _______ index of refraction. As a result, red light is bent _________ violet light. This difference causes light leaving a prism to be dispersed into a(n) _________. Different light sources have different ________, which can be studied by dispersing the light with a prism. Water droplets in the air act as prisms, refracting each color at a(n) ________ angle. In each water droplet, light is _________ as it enters, _________ inside the droplet, and _________ again as it leaves the droplet.

DATE ________ PERIOD ________ NAME ______________________________

CHAPTER 18 Study Guide

Fill in the blanks as you study the chapter.

18.1 MIRRORS

Objects and Their Images in Plane Mirrors

A plane mirror is a(n) ______, smooth surface that reflects light in a(n) _______ way. When light rays are reflected from a plane mirror, they _________. The light rays can be extended _______ the mirror. The image is located where the extended light rays _______________. The image is virtual because there is ______ light at that point. The distance from the object to the mirror is ________ the distance from the image to the mirror. The size of the image is ________ the size of the object. The position of the image is ______, and the ______ and ______ appear to be reversed. Actually, the ______ and ______ are reversed.

Concave Mirrors

A concave mirror reflects light from its ______ surface. In a spherical concave mirror, the center of the sphere is called the ______________. The line from this point to the center of the surface of the mirror is the ___________ of the mirror. Parallel light rays ________ at the focal point, which is ______ the distance between the mirror and the center of curvature. The focal length of a concave mirror is the distance from the _________ to the surface of the mirror, along the ___________. The focal length is ______ the radius of curvature of the mirror.

Spherical Aberration and Parabolic Mirrors

Parallel light rays converge at the focal point if they are close to the ___________ of the mirror. Other parallel light rays converge slightly ________ the mirror. This difference causes the effect known as _______________. To avoid this effect, use a curved mirror that is ________ in shape. These mirrors can also produce a beam of parallel light rays if the source of the light is placed at the _________ of the mirror.

Real vs Virtual Images

An image is real if light rays ________ and then ___________ the image. A real image ______ be projected on a screen. An image is virtual if light rays do not ________, but appear to _______ from a point behind the mirror. A virtual image _______ be projected on a screen.

CHAPTER 18 Study Guide

NAME ______________________________

Real Images Formed by Concave Mirrors

The real image of an object beyond the center of curvature of a concave mirror is located between the ________________ and the __________ of the mirror. The size of the image is ___________ the size of the object, and the position of the image is ________. As the object is moved inward toward the center of curvature, the image moves ________ toward the ________________. If the object is at the center of curvature the real image is at the ________________. The size of the image is ________ the size of the object, and the position of the image is ________. The mirror equation, ____________, can be used to predict the location of an image. In this equation, f represents the ___________, d_i represents the distance from the _______ to the mirror, and d_o represents the distance from the _______ to the mirror. The ratio of the size of the _______ to the size of the _______ is the magnification of the mirror. The magnification equation is ______________. In this equation, _______ represents magnification, d_i and d_o are the same as in the mirror equation, h_i represents the _______________, and h_o represents the _______________. If d_i and d_o are both positive, then both _______ and _______ are negative, which means the position of the image is ________.

Virtual Images Formed by Concave Mirrors

If the object is at the focal point, the reflected rays are ________, and the image is said to be at _______. If the object is between the focal point and the mirror, the _______ image is located _______ the mirror. The size of the image is ____________ the size of the object, and the position of the image is ______.

Virtual Images Formed by Convex Mirrors

A convex mirror reflects light from its _______ surface. Rays reflected from this surface always ________, so they do not form _______ images. The focal point of a convex mirror is located _______ the mirror. In calculations, the focal length of a convex mirror is a(n) ________ number. A convex mirror always produces a(n) _______ image. The size of the image is __________ the size of the object, and the position of the image is ______.

CHAPTER 18 Study Guide

NAME ______________________________

18.2 LENSES

Types of Lenses

A lense is made of a(n) __________ material. The refractive index of the lens material is ________ ______ the refractive index of air. At least one surface of a lens is part of a(n) ________. The other surface may be ________ or it may be _____. A convex lens is ________ at the center than at the edges. A convex lens is called a(n) __________ lens because it refracts parallel rays so that they ______. A concave lens is ________ at the center than at the edges. This lens is called a(n) _________ lens because it refracts light rays so that they __________.

Real Images Formed by Convex Lenses

The principal axis of a lens is a line ____________ to the plane of the lens that passes through its _________. Parallel rays converge at the __________ of the lens. The focal length of the lens depends on its _______ and on the _____________ of the material used to make the lens. Although light is refracted at the two _________ of the lens, lens drawings often show all refraction occurring at the _____________, which passes through the middle of the lens. If the object is far from the convex lens, a(n) ______ image is formed. The size of the image is _________ the size of the object, and the position of the image is _________. If the object is close to, but outside, the focal point of the lens, a(n) ______ image is formed. The size of the image is ___________ the size of the object, and the position of the image is _________. If the object is placed twice the focal length from the lens, the image is at ______ the focal length from the lens. The size of the image is ________ the size of the object and the position of the object is ________. The lens equation is ______________. The magnification equation is ______________.

Virtual Images Formed by Convex Lenses

If the object is placed between the focal point and the lens, the light rays do not __________ on the other side of the lens. The _______ image appears on the ______ side of the lens as the object. The size of the image is ___________ the size of the object, and the position of the image is ______. A convex lens used to produce an enlarged, upright image is called a(n) __________ glass.

Virtual Images Formed by Concave Lenses

A concave lens always causes light rays to ________. A concave lens always produces a(n) _______ image. The size of the image is _________ the size of the object, and the position of the image is ______. The focal length of a concave lens is always a(n) ________ number.

CHAPTER 18 Study Guide

NAME ____________________

Chromatic Aberration

The edges of a lens act like a(n) ______, and bend different ____________ of light at different angles. As a result, light that passes through the edge of the lens is slightly __________, causing a ring of ______ to be seen through the lens. This effect, called chromatic aberration, always occurs when a(n) _______ lens is used. It is reduced by combining a convex lens with a(n) _________ lens that has a(n) _________ index of refraction. A lens made in this way is called a(n) ___________ lens.

Optical Instruments

The eye focuses light on the ______. Most of the refraction in the eye occurs as light enters the ________. The lens of the eye is made of a(n) ________ material that has a different index of refraction than the _____ inside the eye. Tiny muscles in the eye change the _______, and therefore, the focal length of the lens. When the muscles relax, the focal length is _______, and ________ objects can be focused on the retina. When the muscles contract, the focal length becomes ________, and ______ objects can be focused on the retina. If a person is nearsighted, or ________, images of distant objects form ___________ the retina. Nearsightedness is corrected with _________ lenses. If a person is farsighted, images form ________ the retina. Farsightedness is corrected with ________ lenses. If the eye or the lens is not __________, the person has astigmatism. Contact lenses are placed on the ________ and change the focal length of the eye. Microscopes use at least two ________ lenses to focus on small objects. The objective lens has a(n) ______ focal length, and produces a(n) _____ image. The eyepiece lens produces a magnified _______ image of the image formed by the objective lens. A telescope is used to focus on _______ objects. The objective lens has a(n) ______ focal length, and the eyepiece lens has a(n) ______ focal length. The viewer sees a(n) _______ image.

DATE ________ PERIOD ________ NAME ______________________________

CHAPTER 19 Study Guide

Fill in the blanks as you study the chapter.

19.1 WHEN LIGHT WAVES INTERFERE

The Two-Slit Interference Pattern

The edges of shadows are not perfectly ______ because of diffraction, the ________ of light waves around the edges of ________. In Thomas Young's experiment, light passed through two ______ and was diffracted. The overlapping light produced a pattern of ______ and ______ bands. These bands are called interference _______. Monochromatic light is light of only one __________. Monochromatic light that passes through a slit is described as coherent because the waves are all _______. When monochromatic light passes through two slits, __________ interference occurs where crests overlap, producing a(n) ______ band in the pattern. Where a crest and a trough meet, __________ interference occurs, producing a(n) ______ band in the pattern. In this pattern the central band is a(n) ______ band. If white light is used instead of monochromatic light, ________ are seen instead of dark and light bands, and the central band is ______.

Measuring the Wavelength of a Wave

Using double-slit diffraction, _______ measured the wavelength of light. The first bright band on either side of the central band is called the _________ line. It is caused by the __________ interference of two waves the paths of which differ by exactly ____________. The equation used to calculate the wavelength of a light wave is ________. In this equation, ______ represents wavelength, ______ represents the distance between the screen and the slits, ______ represents the distance between the slits, and ______ represents the distance between the central band and the first-order line.

Single-Slit Diffraction

The diffraction of light is less noticeable than the diffraction of sound because the wavelengths of light are _______ than the wavelengths of sound. When light passes through a single slit, the pattern seen has a wide ______ band in the center with ________ bright bands on either side. At the central band, all waves are in step, so __________ interference occurs. To the side of the central band, waves _______ in step, and so __________ interference occurs, producing a dark band. The next bright band is seen when two waves on paths that differ by one __________ meet and __________ interference occurs. The equation used to calculate the wavelength of light is ________. In this equation, ______ represents wavelength, ______ represents the distance from the slit to the screen, ______ represents the width of the slit, ______ represents the distance from the bright band to the dark band. For a constant slit width, the shorter the wavelength, the ________ the pattern.

CHAPTER 19 Study Guide

NAME ______________________________

19.2 APPLICATIONS OF DIFFRACTION

Diffraction Gratings

A diffraction grating is a device that has a series of many _______. On a glass diffraction grating, the _____________ between scratched lines serve as the slits. Compared to double-slit diffraction patterns, the patterns produced by a grating have narrower _______ bands and wider _______ bands. This pattern makes it easier to distinguish individual _______. The equation used to calculate wavelength with a diffraction grating is similar to the ________-slit equation, but the _______ between the central band and first-order line is measured instead of the distance between them. The device used for this measurement is called a grating _____________, and is calibrated so that the _______ can be read directly.

Resolving Power of Lenses

Light passing through the lens of a telescope is __________ by the lens. As a result, the light coming from a star will ___________. If two stars are close together, the light from the stars will ________ and will be seen as one star. According to the Rayleigh criterion for __________, the two images are resolved if the central bright band of one star falls on the __________ band of the second star. The effects of diffraction can be reduced in a telescope by using a(n) _______ lens. The effects of diffraction in a microscope can be reduced by using a light with a(n) ________ wavelength.

DATE ________ PERIOD ________ NAME ____________________

CHAPTER 20 Study Guide

Fill in the blanks as you study the chapter.

20.1 ELECTRICAL CHARGES

Charged Objects

Electrostatics is the study of electrical ________ that can be ________ and held in one place. The force exerted by charged objects is known to be strong because the ________ caused by this force is greater than the acceleration caused by ________ force. The electrical effect and the effect of gravity are different because only the effect of ________ is constant. Two identical objects that have been charged the same way ________ each other. Objects that are charged differently ________ each other. There are two states of charge, called ________ and ________. These charges are produced only in ________. Rubbing two objects together ________ the charges.

A Microscopic View of Charging

An atom contains light, negatively-charged particles called ________, which surround a positively charged ________. The positive charge of the nucleus is exactly ________ by the negative charge of the electrons, so the atom is not ________. The addition of ________ can remove electrons from atoms, leaving behind a(n) ________ ion. If the electrons that were removed become attached to another atom, a(n) ________ ion is produced. If two objects are rubbed together, electrons from one object are ________ to the second. As a result, the first object has a(n) ________ charge and the second object has a(n) ________ charge. The total charge on the two objects is ________ the total charge before they were rubbed together, because charges cannot be ________ or ________. They can only be ________.

Conductors and Insulators

Materials through which charges will not move easily are called electrical ________. Materials that allow charges to move about easily are called electrical ________. Glass is an example of a(n) ________. Metal is an example of a good ________ because at least one ________ in each metal atom is free to move throughout the entire piece of metal. Although air is a(n) ________, it conducts a charge if the ________ exerted by the charges remove ________ from molecules in the air, forming a conductor called ________.

CHAPTER 20 Study Guide

NAME ______________________________

20.2 ELECTRICAL FORCES

Forces on Charged Bodies

The two kinds of electrical charges are ________ and ________. Charges exert ______ on ______ ________ over a distance. ______ charges repel and ______ charges attract. A device called a(n) ____________ is used to detect charges. When a negatively-charged rod touches the knob of the electroscope, _________ are added to the knob, and spread over all the ______ surfaces. The two leaves inside the electroscope become __________ charged, and ______ each other. Charging a neutral body by __________ with a charged body is called charging by conduction. If the electroscope is given a positive charge, the leaves become _________ charged, and ______ each other. To identify the charge on an electroscope, bring an object with known charge ______ the electroscope. If the leaves move farther apart, the charge on the electroscope is ____________ the charge on the object. If the leaves move closer together, the charge on the electroscope is ___________ the charge on the object.

Separation of Charge and Charging by Induction

Electric forces can change insulators into __________. If an uncharged object is brought near a positively charged object, the _________ charges in the uncharged object will be ___________ the positively charged object. The uncharged object will still be _______, but the charges will be _________. Causing charges to separate without touching the object is called charging by _________. The _________ charges on the bottom of thunderclouds can separate ________ in Earth.

Coulomb's Law

Coulomb's law describes the ______ between two charged objects. The electric force varies _________ with the _______ of the distance between the two charged objects. The electric force varies _______ with the ________ of the charges on the objects. Coulomb's law can be written as an equation, ___________. In this equation, F represents ______, q and q' represent the ________ on the objects, d represents the ________ between the objects, and K is a(n) _________. The force that one charged object exerts on a second is _________ the magnitude of the force the second object exerts on the first. The two forces are _________ in direction. This relationship between forces is an example of Newton's ______ law.

CHAPTER 20 Study Guide

NAME ______________________________

The Unit of Charge: The Coulomb

Coulomb defined a(n) __________ quantity of charge in terms of the amount of ______ it produces. The SI unit of ________ is the Coulomb, abbreviated as ______. One coulomb is the charge of 6.25×10^{18} __________. The magnitude of the charge of one electron is called the __________ charge. The electric force is a(n) _______ quantity, which means it has both __________ and _________. A repulsive force has a(n) ________ sign and an attractive force has a(n) _________ sign.

Using Electric Forces on Neutral Bodies

A charged object may either _______ or _______ another charged object. A charged object may only _______ an uncharged object. The uncharged object will then _______ the charged object. This relationship is an example of Newton's ______ law. Electric forces are used to collect ________ particles such as soot in smokestacks.

DATE ________ PERIOD ________ NAME ________________________________

CHAPTER 21 Study Guide

Fill in the blanks as you study the chapter.

21.1 CREATING AND MEASURING ELECTRIC FIELDS

The Electric Field

A(n) ________ produces an electric field. The electric field can be observed because it produces ________ on other ________. An electric field is measured by placing a small ________ test charge in it. According to ____________ law, the force is proportional to the test charge. The equation used to calculate the magnitude of an electric field is ______. In this equation, ______ represents the magnitude of the field, ______ represents the force on the test charge, and ______ represents the magnitude of the test charge. The magnitude of the field is a(n) ______, because it has both magnitude and ________. The direction of the electric field is ____________ the direction of the force on the positive test charge. The magnitude of the intensity of an electric field is measured in ____________________. To measure the entire field, the ____________ is moved to locations throughout the field until all locations have been tested. The total electric field is the vector ______ of the fields of the individual charges.

Picturing the Electric Field

When electric field lines are used to show a field, the direction of the field at any point is the ________ drawn to the field line at that point. The ________ of the field is indicated by the spacing between the lines, and is ________ where the lines are closer together. Near a positive charge, the direction of the force on a positive test charge is __________ the positive charge. Near a negative charge, the direction of the force on a positive test charge is ________ the charge. Field lines ________ exist, but electric fields ______ exist. The field provides a way of calculating the ______ on a charged body. It does not explain why ________ bodies exert ______ on each other.

CHAPTER 21 Study Guide

NAME ______________________________

21.2 APPLICATIONS OF THE ELECTRIC FIELD

Energy and the Electric Potential

Two unlike charges ______ each other, so work must be done to move them ___________. When work is done on the charges, it is stored as ________ energy. The potential energy of a test charge is called the electric _________, and is measured in a unit called the ______. The change in potential energy per unit _______ is called the electric potential difference. When work is done to move a positive test charge farther from a(n) ________ charge, the potential energy of the test charge increases. When the positive test charge is moved back to its original position, its potential energy __________. Only __________ in electric potential energy can be measured. Potential differences are measured with a(n) _________. When a positive test charge is moved away from a positive charge, the potential energy __________. The electric potential is ________ when the positive test charge is closest to the positive charge.

The Electric Potential in a Uniform Field

The electric field between two _______ plates is uniform. The equation used to calculate the potential difference between two points in a uniform field is ________. In this equation, ______ represents the potential difference, ______ represents the magnitude of the field, and ______ represents the distance between the points.

Millikan's Oil Drop Experiment

The measurement of the charge of a(n) ________ was made by Robert A. Millikan. In this experiment, fine drops of oil were sprayed by a(n) ________ into the ______. The drops were charged by _______ as they passed through the _________. The drops fell due to _______. Some of the drops were trapped between two charged parallel _______. The potential difference between the plates was adjusted until a charged drop was __________ between the plates. At this point the __________ force of the weight of the drop was ________ the ________ force of the electric field. Although the drops had a wide variety of charges, the ________ in the charge were always a multiple of -1.6×10^{-19} C. Millikan concluded that this was the ________ change in charge that could occur, and was equal to the charge of one ________.

Sharing of Charge

All systems come to __________ when the energy of the system is at a minimum. In an electrical system, this happens when all objects in the system have the same _________. In a conductor, charges _______ until all parts of the conductor have the same potential. If a large sphere and a small sphere have the same charge, the larger sphere will have the ______ potential, because charges are ______ spread out on the larger surface area. If the spheres are touched together, charge will move from the _______

NAME ____________________

sphere to the ______ sphere, until their potentials are equal. When the two spheres are at the same potential, the ______ sphere will have the greater charge. Because Earth is such a large sphere, almost any amount of charge can flow into it without changing its ________. Thus Earth can absorb ______ charges from an object, which is called _________ the object.

Electric Fields Near Conductors

The charges on a conductor spread out as far as possible, which makes the energy of the system as ______ as possible. If a conductor is solid, all the charges are on the _______. If a conductor is hollow, all charges move to the ______ surface. A closed metal container _______ the inside from electric fields. Charges are ____________ at sharp points of a conductor, and the field is ________ at these points. A lightning rod has a(n) _______ shape so that lightning will strike the rod rather than the house. From the rod, the charges flow to the _______.

Storing Charges—The Capacitor

As charge is added to an object, the potential between the object and ______ increases. The ratio of charge to potential difference is a constant, called the __________ of the object. A device that is designed to have a specific __________ is called a capacitor. A capacitor is used to store _______. In the capacitor there are two __________ separated by a(n) ________. The conductors have equal and opposite ________. Capacitance is __________ of the charge placed on the capacitor. The equation used to calculate capacitance is ________. In this equation, ______ represents capacitance, ______ represents the charge on one plate, and ______ represents the potential difference between the plates. The unit used to measure capacitance is the ______. One coulomb per ______ is equal to one farad.

DATE ________ PERIOD ________ NAME ____________________

CHAPTER 22 Study Guide

Fill in the blanks as you study the chapter.

22.1 CURRENT AND CIRCUITS

Producing Electric Current

When two conducting spheres at different potentials are allowed to touch, ________ flow from the object at the ________ potential to the object at the ________ potential. This flow continues until the potentials are ________. The flow of ________ particles is called an electric current. In some conductors, negatively charged ________ move. In other conductors, positively charged ________ move. To keep the flow of charges moving, there must be a(n) ________ difference, which can be maintained by pumping ________ from one conductor to another. The pumping process would increase the electric ________ energy of the particles, so it would require a(n) ________ source of energy. A voltaic cell converts ________ energy to electric energy. A photovoltaic cell converts ________ energy into electric energy. A generator converts ________ energy into electric energy.

Electric Circuits

A(n) ________ loop through which charges move is called an electric circuit. The circuit includes a charge pump that ________ the potential energy of the charges, and a device that ________ the potential energy of the charges. This device converts ________ energy to another form of energy. A motor converts electric energy to ________ energy. A lamp converts electric energy to ________ energy. A heater converts electric energy to ________ energy. Charged particles lose electric ________ as they flow through such devices, and these devices are said to have ________. The total amount of ________ in a circuit does not change, so charge is a(n) ________ quantity. The net change in potential energy of the charges going around the circuit is ________.

Rates of Charge Flow and Energy Transfer

The rate at which energy is transferred is ________. The energy carried by an electric current depends on the ________ transferred and the ________ across which it moves. Electric ________ is measured in amperes. A device that measures current is called a(n) ________. The flow of ________ charge is called conventional current. The equation used to calculate the power of an electric device is ________. In this equation, ________ represents power, ________ represents potential difference, and ________ represents the current.

CHAPTER 22 Study Guide

NAME ______________________________

Resistance and Ohm's Law

The property that determines how much _______ will flow in a conductor is resistance. Resistance is measured by placing a potential difference across _______ points on a conductor, and measuring the _______ that flows. The equation that defines resistance is _______. Resistance is measured in _______. If the resistance of a conductor does not depend on the _______ or _________ of the potential difference across it, the resistance is said to obey _______ law. A(n) ________ is a device that is designed to have a specific resistance. A superconductor is a material that has a resistance of _______, and can conduct electricity without a(n) _______ of energy. Current in a circuit can be controlled by varying either the ________________ or the ___________, or both. To produce a smooth, continuous variation in current, a variable ________ called a(n) _____________ is used.

Diagramming Circuits

A circuit _________, or schematic, is drawn using standard _________ to represent the elements of the _______. When a schematic is drawn, the symbol for the source of electric energy is drawn so that the ________ terminal is at the top. A wire following the ____________ current is drawn out of this terminal, and the path is followed until the ________ terminal of the source of energy is reached. An ammeter is connected to a circuit in a(n) _______ connection and a voltmeter is connected in a(n) _______ connection.

CHAPTER 22 Study Guide

NAME ______________________________

22.2 USING ELECTRICAL ENERGY

Energy Transfer in Electric Circuits

A capacitor is used to _______ electric energy. When the capacitor is uncharged, the potential difference across it is _______. If a capacitor is connected to a battery through a resistor, _________ will flow to the _________. At first the current will be ______, but as the voltage across the capacitor increases, the current will _________ until the voltage across the capacitor is ________ the voltage across the battery. At this point the capacitor is _________. The capacitor discharges when it is connected across a(n) ________. Current will flow until the voltage across the capacitor is _______. The electric energy stored in the capacitor is changed to ________ energy at the resistor. Electric power is the energy per unit _______ converted by an electric _______ into another form of energy. The equation used to calculate power is _________. If all the electric energy is converted into thermal energy, the energy transferred is the product of _______ and ______. The equation used to calculate the increase in thermal energy is __________.

Transmission of Electric Energy

If electricity is to be transmitted over long distances, there will be a _______ of energy as electric energy is converted to ________ energy. To reduce this loss, there is little that can be done to reduce the __________ of the wires. However, it is possible to reduce the ________ by increasing the ________.

The Kilowatt Hour

The electric energy used by a device is the product of its _______ and the _______ it is operated. The joule is equal to one ______ of power per ________, and is a very small unit. The unit more commonly used is the ____________. If 1000 watts of power are delivered continuously for one hour, one ____________ of energy is used.

DATE ________ PERIOD ________ NAME ______________________________

CHAPTER 23 Study Guide

Fill in the blanks as you study the chapter.

23.1 SIMPLE CIRCUITS

Series Circuits

In a series circuit, resistors are connected so that all ________ flows through each resistor. There is only one _______ for the current in the circuit. The current in each device is _________ the current in the generator. The increase in potential energy across the __________ is equal to the total potential drop, which is equal to the _______ of the potential drops around the rest of the circuit. The total resistance, or ___________ resistance, is the _______ of the individual resistances in the circuit. The equivalent resistance in a series circuit is ____________ the resistance of any one device in the circuit. After the total resistance and total voltage drops have been found, the current in the circuit can be found using the equation ______.

Voltage Drops in a Series Circuit

The battery or generator in a circuit __________ the potential and the resistors __________ the potential. These two changes are _______, and the net change around the circuit is _______. The potential drop across any one resistor in a series circuit is determined by finding the ___________________ in the circuit and using this to find the current. Once the current is known, this value and the resistance of the individual device are __________ to find the potential drop across the device. A voltage divider is a simple _______ circuit that uses an extra ________ to adjust the potential in the circuit.

Parallel Circuits

A parallel circuit has __________ one path for the current. The total current is the _______ of the currents moving through each path. The potential difference across one of the paths is _________ the potential difference across the other paths. Each path acts as if the other paths _________ present. In a parallel circuit, the equivalent resistance is _________ the resistance of any individual resistor. If you add another resistor in parallel, the equivalent resistance __________. The reciprocal of the equivalent resistance is equal to the _______ of the reciprocals of the individual resistors.

CHAPTER 23 Study Guide

NAME ______________________________

23.2 APPLICATIONS OF CIRCUITS

Safety Devices

Fuses and circuit breakers are ________ that are used as safety devices that prevent a current ________. Most homes use ________ circuits. If several appliances are in use at once, the resistance of each appliance ________ the total resistance of the circuit, which ________ the current. The current in an appliance is found by using the equation _____. In this equation, P represents the power rating in ______, which is marked on the appliance. Once the current is known, the resistance of each appliance can be calculated, using the equation ______. After the ________ resistance for all appliances has been calculated, the total current can be found. If the total current is ________ the rating of the fuse, the fuse will open the circuit. A short circuit occurs when a circuit with a very low ________ forms. Such a circuit carries a very high ________, which could produce enough ______ to start a fire.

Combined Series-Parallel Circuits

The first step in analyzing a combined circuit is to calculate the ________ resistance of all resistors that are connected in ________. If any of the equivalent resistances are now connected in ______, calculate their equivalent resistance. Repeat these two steps until the entire circuit has been reduced to ______ equivalent resistance. Next, calculate the ________ in the circuit. Finally, calculate the ________ and currents through individual resistors.

Ammeters and Voltmeters

An ammeter measures the ________ in a part of a circuit, and should be connected in ______ with the resistance. An ammeter should not change the ________ of the circuit, so it should have the lowest possible ________. A voltmeter measures the ________ across some part of a circuit, and should be connected in ________ with the resistor. A voltmeter should not change the ________ or ________ ______ in a circuit, so it should have a high ________.

DATE ________ PERIOD ________ NAME ______________________________

CHAPTER 24 Study Guide

Fill in the blanks as you study the chapter.

24.1 MAGNETS: PERMANENT AND TEMPORARY

General Properties of Magnets

Each end of a magnet is called a(n) ______. The north-seeking end of a magnet is the ______ pole and the south-seeking end of a magnet is the ______ pole. Two like magnetic poles ______ each other and two unlike magnetic poles ______ each other. If an object becomes polarized when it is near a magnet, the object has become a(n) ________ magnet. The direction of ________ of a temporary magnet depends on the polarization of the ________ magnet. When the permanent magnet is taken away from the temporary magnet, the temporary magnet will ______ its magnetism.

Magnetic Fields Around Permanent Magnets

The forces between magnets occur when the magnets ______ each other and when they are at a(n) ________. Iron filings can show the __________ around a magnet because each filing that is near the magnet becomes a(n) ________. The filing rotates until it is ________ to the magnetic field at that point. Magnetic field lines can be used to show the ________ of a magnetic field. The number of magnetic field lines passing through a surface is the __________. The ______ per unit area is proportional to the ________ of the magnetic field. The flux lines are most concentrated near the ______ of the magnet. The direction of the field lines is the direction to which the ______ of a compass points when it is placed in the field. Magnetic field lines do not have ends, so they form ______. The field lines between two ______ poles run directly between the poles. The magnetic field of one magnet can exert a(n) ______ on a second magnet, causing it to become ________ with the field. When a sample of iron is placed near a magnet, the field lines are __________ in the sample of iron. The end of the iron sample nearest the N-pole of the magnet becomes the ______ of the sample, and the sample ________ the magnet. A superconductor ______ a magnet because there is no __________ inside the superconductor.

Electromagnetism

When current flows through a wire, it exerts ______ on the poles of a magnet in a direction that is __________ the direction of the current. When there is no current flowing in the wire, no ______ is exerted on a magnet. The magnetic field lines around a wire that is carrying current form a pattern of ________ circles, with the ______ at the center of each circle. The strength of the magnetic field around a long, straight wire is proportional to the ______ in the wire. The strength varies ________

NAME ______________________________

with the distance from the wire. When the direction of current is reversed, the ________ of the magnetic field is reversed. According to the first right-hand rule, if your _______ points in the direction of the conventional current, the fingers of your hand circle the ______ and point in the ________ of the magnetic field.

Magnetic Field Near a Coil

When a current flows through a coil of wire, the field around all the loops will have the same ________. The field around the coil is similar to the field around a(n) ________________, and the coil has a(n) _______ pole and a(n) _______ pole. Because the coil acts like a(n) ________, it is called an electromagnet. According to the second right-hand rule, if your _______ point in the direction of conventional current in the coil, your _______ points toward the N-pole of the electromagnet. The field of an electromagnet becomes ________ when an iron core is placed inside the coil because the core becomes __________ by induction. The strength of the field around an electromagnet is proportional to the ________ of current in the coil and the number of ______ in the coil. It also depends on the _______ of the core.

A Microscopic Picture of Magnetic Materials

Magnetism in a permanent magnet is the result of the magnetic fields of ________. The fields of groups of atoms called ________ act together. If a piece of iron is not magnetized, the domains point in ________ directions, and their fields _______ each other. A magnetic field causes the domains to ______ with the field. If the domains remain aligned after the magnetic field is removed, the object is a(n) __________ magnet. If the domains lose their alignment, the object is a(n) __________ magnet.

CHAPTER 24 Study Guide

NAME ______________________________

24.2 FORCES CAUSED BY MAGNETIC FIELDS

Forces on Currents in Magnetic Fields

The force on a wire in a magnetic field is ____________ to the direction of the magnetic field and also is ____________ to the direction of the current. According to the third right-hand rule, if your _______ point in the direction of the magnetic field and your _______ points in the direction of the conventional current, the ______ of your hand faces in the direction of the force acting on the wire. When the currents in two wires flow in the same direction, the wires _______ each other. If the currents flow in opposite directions, the wires ______ each other.

Measuring the Force on a Wire Due to a Magnetic Field

The magnitude of the force acting on a current-carrying wire in a magnetic field is proportional to the ________ of the field, the amount of _______ in the wire, and the _______ of the wire that is in the field. The strength of a magnetic field is called magnetic _________, and is measured in _______. One tesla is equivalent to one ________ per ____________.

Galvanometers

A galvanometer is used to measure very small ________. It contains a small coil of _______ placed in the strong field of a(n) __________ magnet. Current passing through the loop causes it to _______, which moves a needle in the galvanometer. The amount of rotation of the needle is proportional to the ________. A galvanometer can be converted to a(n) _________ if a resistor with less resistance than the galvanometer is connected in ________ with the galvanometer. A galvanometer can be converted to a(n) _________ if a resistor, called a multiplier, is connected in _______ with the galvanometer.

Electric Motors

The force on a(n) ______________ loop of wire in a magnetic field causes it to ______ through 180°. If the current is _________ at the right time, the loop of wire _______. The current is reversed by a device called a split-ring ___________. The loops of wire in an electric motor make up the _________. The force acting on the armature is proportional to the number of _______ of wire and the _______ of wire in each loop. The force also is proportional to the amount of ________ in the wire, and this variable can be used to change the _______ of the motor.

The Force on a Single Charged Particle

Charged particles can move in wires and also in any region from which the _______ has been removed. In a cathode-ray tube, ____________ pull electrons off atoms in the _________ electrode. Then electric fields gather, __________, and focus the electrons into a narrow _______, which is deflected by ______________. When the electron beam strikes the screen, __________ on the screen glow, producing an image. The force exerted on an electron by a magnetic field depends on the ________ of the electron, the ________ of the field, and the ______ between the directions of the velocity and the field.

DATE ________ PERIOD ________ NAME ____________________________

CHAPTER 25 Study Guide

Fill in the blanks as you study the chapter.

25.1 CREATING ELECTRIC CURRENT FROM CHANGING MAGNETIC FIELDS

Faraday's Discovery

If a wire that is part of a closed ______ moves in one direction through a magnetic field, current flows in ______ direction. If the wire moves in the opposite direction, the ______ moves in the opposite direction. No current flows if the wire is held ________ or moved ________ the magnetic field. To produce a current there must be ______ motion between the wire and the magnetic field. The process of generating a(n) ______ in a wire in a(n) ________ field is electromagnetic induction.

Electromotive Force

The potential difference, or ______, given to charges by a charge pump is called the electromotive ______. The ______ is the unit used to measure *EMF*. When a wire is moved through a magnetic field, a(n) ______ acts on electrons, which move in the ________ of the force. Because ______ is done on the electrons, their ________ energy is increased. The difference in potential is the ________ *EMF*. If a wire moves through a field at an angle to the field, only the component of the motion that is ____________ the direction of the field generates *EMF*.

Electric Generators

The electric generator converts __________ energy to electric energy. The generator consists of wire ______ placed in a strong ________ field. The wire is wound around a core of ______, and together these parts are called the ________. When the armature turns in the field, the wire loops cut through the magnetic field ______, and induce an *EMF*, commonly called ______. If the number of loops on the armature is increased, the *EMF* is ________. As the loop rotates, the ________ and ________ of the current change. Each time the loop turns through ______, the current reverses direction. A motor is like a generator, but the energy conversion is in the ________ direction, changing electric energy to __________ energy.

Alternating Current Generator

A(n) ______ source turns the armature of a generator in a(n) ________ field a fixed number of revolutions per second. In the United States, the current changes through a full cycle ______ times each second, giving the current a frequency of ______. The power produced by a generator is the product of the ______ and the ______. Because these quantities vary, power varies, and is usually described in terms of the ________ power. The voltage available at electric outlets is the ________ voltage, not the ________ voltage.

CHAPTER 25 Study Guide

NAME ____________________

25.2 EFFECTS OF CHANGING MAGNETIC FIELDS: INDUCED *EMF*

Lenz's Law

According to Lenz's law, the ________ of the induced current is such that the magnetic field resulting from the induced current opposes the change in ______ that caused the induced current. As a result, a generator that is producing _______ is subject to a force that opposes the turning of the ________ of the generator. As the current being generated increases, the magnitude of the opposing force ________. In a motor, a similar effect produces _________, which is in the opposite direction to the flow of current. A mechanical load placed on the motor _________ the net current flowing through the motor, and _________ the back-*EMF*.

Self-Inductance

Current generates a(n) _________ field, creating new field ______, which cut through the wires. As a result, an *EMF* is generated and it opposes the current _______. The faster you try to change the current, the ______ the opposing *EMF*, and the ______ the current change. Because of this self-inductance, ______ has to be done to increase the _______ that flows, and _______ is stored in the magnetic field.

Transformers

A transformer is used to increase or decrease AC ________ without a loss of _______. A transformer contains two ______ that are insulated electrically from each other, but that share the same ______. When the primary coil is connected to a source of AC _______, the changing current creates a varying ________ field. A varying _______ is induced in the secondary coil, by the process of _______ inductance. The ratio of the primary and secondary ________ depends on the ratio of the number of turns in the two ______. In a step-up transformer, the primary voltage is _________ the secondary voltage, and the current in the primary circuit is ___________ the current in the secondary. In a step-down transformer, the primary voltage is ___________ the secondary voltage and the current in the primary circuit is _________ the current in the secondary circuit.

DATE ________ PERIOD ________ NAME ______________________________

CHAPTER 26 Study Guide

Fill in the blanks as you study the chapter.

26.1 ACTION OF ELECTRIC AND MAGNETIC FIELDS ON MATTER

Mass of the Electron

The mass of an electron can be calculated from the ratio of ________ to ________. In a cathode-ray tube, crossed ________ and ________ fields exert forces on electrons. The forces exerted by the two fields act in ________ directions. The electric field deflects electrons upward, and the magnetic field deflects electrons ________. The electrons travel in a straight line when the forces due to the fields are equal in ________ and opposite in ________. When the electric field is turned off, the magnetic field causes a(n) ________ acceleration on the electrons, and the electrons are deflected off the straight path. The amount of deflection indicates the charge-to-mass ________. If the electric field is reversed, the same process can be used to find the mass of ________ particles.

The Mass Spectrometer

In a mass spectrometer, gas ions with a(n) ________ charge are produced. A(n) ________ field accelerates the ions, which pass through deflecting ________ and ________ fields. The ions strike a piece of ________ film. Each ________ of the element makes a mark in a different spot on the film. Because all of the ions in the spectrometer have the same charge, the difference in deflection is due to differences in the ________ of the isotopes. If containers are used in place of the film, the isotopes can be ________ and saved.

CHAPTER 26 Study Guide

NAME ____________________

26.2 ELECTRIC AND MAGNETIC FIELDS IN SPACE

Electromagnetic Waves

Changing magnetic fields induce changing ________ fields that are made up of closed _______. Changing electric fields induce changing _________ fields, even if there are no ________ present. Combined electric and magnetic _______ that move through _______ are called electromagnetic waves. These waves move at the speed of _______. When an antenna is connected to a source of alternating current, the current generates a(n) _________ magnetic field that moves ________ from the antenna. The electric and magnetic fields are at _______ angles to each other and to the ________ of the motion of the wave. The electric field is ________ to the direction of the antenna wires.

Production of Electromagnetic Waves

The __________ of the electromagnetic waves can be changed by varying the speed at which the generator is rotated. The frequencies of radio and television waves are _______ than the frequencies that can be produced by a turning generator. These frequencies are produced by the combination of a(n) _______ and a(n) _________. The frequency depends on the _______ of the capacitor and the coil. Both the _________ field of the coil and the ________ field of the capacitor contain ________. When the current is large, the magnetic field has the _________ amount of energy, and the capacitor has the _______ amount of energy. When the current is _______, then all the energy is in the electric field of the _________. As the energy moves between the electric and magnetic fields, ________ is added in the form of ________ pulses. These pulses can also be produced by quartz ________, which generate a(n) ______ when they are bent. Quartz crystals are useful because they produce a(n) ________ frequency.

Reception of Electromagnetic Waves

When electromagnetic waves strike an antenna, they __________ electrons in the antenna. This effect is greatest when the antenna is ________ to the direction of the ________ fields of the wave. A(n) _______ in the antenna oscillates at the frequency of the electromagnetic wave. If the length of the antenna is ________ the wavelength of the wave, the antenna __________. The antenna is connected to a(n) _______ and a(n) _________. The capacitance is adjusted until the frequency of the _______ equals the frequency of the desired wave. In this way, the device will amplify only one __________.

X Rays

X rays are ______________ electromagnetic waves, produced when _________ are accelerated to high speeds. When the high-speed electrons strike matter, their _______ energies are converted into electromagnetic _______. X rays can be produced by ___________ tubes. In a television set, the glass front of the tube contains _______, which absorbs the X rays.

DATE ________ PERIOD ______ NAME ______________________________

CHAPTER 27 Study Guide

Fill in the blanks as you study the chapter.

27.1 WAVES BEHAVE LIKE PARTICLES

Radiation From Incandescent Bodies

An incandescent object gives off light of all ______ as well as ______ radiation. A spectrum is a plot of the ______ of radiation emitted at various ______. Light and radiation are produced by the ______ of ______ particles within atoms of a hot body. The ______ at which the maximum amount of light is emitted is proportional to the temperature on the ______ scale. The total power emitted increases with ______. Max Planck assumed that atoms could vibrate only at specific ______, and that the energy of vibration is ______. Planck also suggested that an atom could emit radiation only when the vibration energy ______.

Photoelectric Effect

The emission of ______ when electromagnetic ______ falls on an object is called the photoelectric effect. The emission of electrons causes a(n) ______ to flow in a circuit. Electrons are emitted only if the ______ of the radiation is above a minimum value, or ______ frequency. Radiation of a frequency below the threshold value does not ______ any electrons from a metal. Once the threshold frequency is reached, the greater the ______ of radiation, and the larger the flow of photoelectrons. Light and other forms of radiation consist of photons, which are discrete bundles of ______. The energy of the photon depends on the ______ of the light. To eject an electron, a photon must have a minimum amount of ______. If the photon has more than the minimum amount of energy, the excess energy becomes the ______ energy of the ______. The threshold frequency is related to the energy needed to free the most ______ electron from a metal. This amount of energy is called the ______ function of the metal.

The Compton Effect

Although it has no ______, a photon has ______ energy just as a particle does. Einstein predicted that the photon should have a second particle property, ______. The momentum of a photon is ______ proportional to the wavelength. Arthur Compton found that some X rays lose ______ when they strike matter and are scattered with ______ wavelengths than the original X rays. The increase in ______ when X rays are scattered off of ______ is called the Compton effect. Compton also showed that photons obey the law of ______ of momentum and conservation of ______.

CHAPTER 27 Study Guide

NAME ______________________________

27.2 PARTICLES BEHAVE LIKE WAVES

Matter Waves

Particles such as ________ or protons show wavelike _________. If a beam of _________ is aimed at a crystal, the atoms in the crystal act as a(n) ______________. The diffraction of the electrons forms the same pattern as diffraction of _______ of a similar wavelength. The wavelength of a particle is the __________ wavelength, and is too ______ to produce observable effects.

Particles and Waves

A(n) ________ is usually described in terms of mass, size, kinetic energy, and momentum. A(n) ______ is usually described in terms of frequency, wavelength, and amplitude. Because of its length, a wave cannot be located at one ______ in space. Most scientists believe that the particle and wave aspects of light should be studied ________. To find the location of a(n) ________, light must be reflected from it. The spreading out of light due to _________ makes it impossible to locate a particle exactly. If light of a(n) _______ wavelength is used, there is less diffraction. However, because of the ________ effect, the short-wavelength light changes the __________ of the particle. Thus, measuring the ________ of a particle changes its momentum. Similarly, measuring the momentum changes the ________ of the particle. As a result, the __________ and ________ of a particle cannot be precisely known at the same _______. This statement is the Heisenberg __________ principle, which is the result of the _______ wave and particle description of light and _______.

DATE ________ PERIOD ________ NAME ____________________

CHAPTER 28 Study Guide

Fill in the blanks as you study the chapter.

28.1 THE BOHR MODEL

The Nuclear Model

Rutherford probed ______ with massive, high-speed particles that had a(n) ________ charge. These particles are now called ______ particles. Rutherford aimed these particles at a thin sheet of metal, and found that ______ of the particles passed through the sheet. A few of the particles were deflected at ______ angles. These results are explained by the fact that the nucleus of an atom contains nearly all the ______ of the atom. All of the ________ charge is also in the nucleus. __________ are outside the nucleus, and the atom is made up mostly of ____________.

Atomic Spectra

The set of wavelengths of light emitted by an atom is the atom's _________ spectrum. When a substance is vaporized in a flame it gives off light that is characteristic of the atoms of the _________ that make up the substance. Atoms in a gas at low _________ emit light when a high ________ is applied across the gas. The spectrum can be studied through a(n) __________ grating. The spectrum can also be studied with a(n) _____________, in which light passes through a(n) _______, then a grating, and then a lens system. The spectrum of a(n) _____________ solid is a continuous band of colors. The spectrum of a(n) _____ is a series of bright lines, one for each ___________ of light given off by the atoms in the gas. When light passes through a gas that is cool, the gas will ________ light at characteristic ____________, forming a(n) ___________ spectrum. The wavelengths that are absorbed by atoms in a cool gas are ____________ the wavelengths the atoms give off when they are excited.

The Bohr Model of the Atom

Rutherford described an atom in which _________ orbited the nucleus much as planets orbit the ______. This planetary model did not account for the fact that no radiation is ________ as electrons move around the nucleus. It also did not account for the fact that atoms emit light only at specific ____________. Bohr suggested that an electron in a stable orbit does not radiate ________, even though the electron is ____________. Light is emitted when the ________ of an electron changes. An electron can absorb only certain amounts of ________. Thus the energy of an electron in an atom is __________. The different amounts of energy that an electron can have are the energy _______, the lowest of which is the ________ state. If an electron absorbs ________, it moves to a(n) ________ state. This condition lasts a very short time, and the electron returns to the ________ state. During this change, the electron emits a(n) ________.

CHAPTER 28 Study Guide

NAME ______________________________

Predictions of the Bohr Model

The Bohr model correctly predicted the ________ spectrum for the element __________, but not for the next element, _______. In his model, Bohr suggested that the angular ___________ of an electron can have only certain values. Thus angular momentum is __________. In addition, the radius of a(n) _____ and the _______ of the electron can have only certain values, and are __________. The principal ________ number determines the radius of the orbit and energy of the ________.

CHAPTER 28 Study Guide

NAME ______________________________

28.2 THE PRESENT MODEL OF THE ATOM

A Quantum Model of the Atom

The quantization of the ________ momentum of an electron is related to the fact that particles show some properties of _______. Because the ________ and ___________ of a particle cannot both be known at the same time, the quantum model of the atom predicts only the __________ that an electron is at a given location. The region in which there is a(n) _______ probability of finding an electron is the electron _______. This model is the basis for quantum ___________, which allows scientists to determine the structure of atoms and __________.

Lasers

Because the light emitted by a(n) _____________ source is at many wavelengths and moving in all directions, the light is described as ___________. When an atom in an excited state is struck by a photon with the correct amount of ________, the atom will emit another photon. The two photons will have the same ___________ and will be in step with each other. In a laser, a flash of light with a(n) ________ wavelength than that of the laser is used to excite _______. As the atoms decay to a(n) ______ state, they lase, or give off ______. As photons are produced, they strike other _______, which then give off more _________. The photons are trapped inside a tube and only a few photons leave through a ________ reflecting mirror. Because all the photons are in step, laser light is described as _________. Because the beam is small, the light is also very ________. The light is all one wavelength, or ______________. Laser light can be carried through glass fibers because the light undergoes total _______________.

DATE ________ PERIOD ________ NAME ____________________________

CHAPTER 29 Study Guide

Fill in the blanks as you study the chapter.

29.1 CONDUCTION IN SOLIDS

Band Theory of Solids

In a(n) __________, electrical charges can move easily. In a(n) _________, charges remain where they are placed. In a single atom, electrons are usually in the _______ possible energy level. When atoms are brought together, their individual ________ fields affect each other, and change the ________ levels. In one atom the energy levels are raised, and in the other atom they are _________. When many atoms are together in a(n) _______ object, no two atoms have the _______ energy levels. The many levels are spread into _______, which are separated by values that are called ______________ because atoms are not allowed to have these energies. In conductors, the _______ band is only partially filled.

Conductors

When a potential difference is placed across a material, the resulting ________ field exerts a(n) _______ on electrons. The electrons are ___________ and they gain ________. This change allows them to move into a(n) _______ energy level. In conductors, the bands are only ________ filled, so there is a higher level into which the electrons can move. As electrons gain energy from the electric _______, they move from one _______ to the next. The free electrons in a conductor move ________ in ________ directions. An electric field placed across a conductor exerts a(n) _______ on the electrons, which still move _________, but drift toward the ________ end of the conductor. This description of a conductor is the ____________ model. If the temperature is increased, the speed of the electrons __________, but the electrons are more likely to _______ with a nucleus. As a result, an increase in temperature causes a decrease in ___________ and an increase in __________.

Insulators

In an insulator, all energy levels in the _______ band are filled. The next available energy level is in a(n) _______ band. If an electron is to be moved through an insulator, it must receive enough energy to remove it from the lowest, or ________, band. Most electric fields do not have enough energy to move electrons from this band to the ___________ band. In an insulator, the __________ gap between the bands is very _______, and few electrons can be moved across it.

Semiconductors

In a semiconductor, electrons move ______ freely than in insulators, but _______ freely than in conductors. Most semiconductors have _______ valence electrons, which are involved in ________ atoms into a crystal structure. The valence electrons fill a(n) ______ but the _____________ between the valence

NAME ________________________________

and conduction bands is smaller than it is in a(n) ________. Very little ________ is needed to move an electron into the ___________ band. As the temperature of the semiconductor increases, _______ electrons are moved into the conduction band. In a semiconductor, as temperature increases, ___________ increases. An atom from which a(n) ________ has broken free contains a hole, or an empty ________ level in the ________ band. The hole has a(n) ________ charge, and a(n) ________ can move into it. Although this hole is filled, the electron that filled it leaves behind a(n) _______ in another atom. The electrons and the holes move in ________ directions. A semiconductor that develops holes because of ________ energy is a(n) ________ semiconductor, and has a low conductivity and a high __________.

Doped Semiconductors

The conductivity of a semiconductor can be increased if impurities called _________ semiconductors are added. These dopants add extra _________ or _______ to the semiconductor. If an atom with five valence electrons replaces an atom with four valence electrons, there is _______ electron that is not needed in _________. This extra, or _______ electron can be moved into the conduction band by a small amount of ________ energy. The semiconductor that conducts by means of _________ is called a(n) _______ semiconductor because it conducts by particles with a(n) _________ charge. If an atom with three valence electrons replaces an atom with four, an extra _______ is formed. Because an electron can move into the hole, the atom is called an electron _________. This type of semiconductor is called a(n) _______ semiconductor. In either type of semiconductor, the net charge on the semiconductor is _______.

CHAPTER 29 Study Guide

NAME ______________________________

29.2 ELECTRONIC DEVICES

Diodes

A diode consists of adjacent regions of ________ and ________ semiconductors. The boundary between the two regions is called the ________. Charges move until the n-side has a net ________ charge, and the p-side has a net ________ charge. Forces between these charges stop the movement of charges in the ________ layer. If the n-type end of a diode is connected to the positive terminal of a battery, both free electrons and holes are attracted toward the battery and the depletion layer is ________. In this reverse-biased diode there is a very large ________ and a very ________ current. If the battery is connected in the opposite way, charge carriers move toward the ________ in the diode, making the ________ layer smaller, and current flows. This forward-biased diode can be used to change ________ current to current with only one ________. When electrons reach the holes at the junction in ________ diodes, or LEDs, the excess ________ is released as light. If the semiconductor crystal is shaped in such a way that light reflects inside the crystal, the diode becomes a(n) ________. A reverse-biased diode can be used as a light ________.

Transistors and Integrated Circuits

In a transistor, there are ________ layers of doped ________. The ________ layer, or base, is different from the two outer layers, which are called the ________ and the ________. In an npn transistor, the potential difference between the collector and emitter is ________. The base-collector junction acts as a(n) ________ diode, so no current flows. The base-emitter junction acts as a(n) ________ diode. A small current through the base-emitter junction produces a(n) ________ current through the base-collector junction. The transistor increases, or ________, voltage changes. In a pnp resistor, the battery potentials are ________, and current is carried by ________.

DATE ________ PERIOD ________ NAME ____________________________

CHAPTER 30 Study Guide

Fill in the blanks as you study the chapter.

30.1 RADIOACTIVITY

Description of the Nucleus

The ________ charge of an atom is found in the nucleus. The positively-charged particle found in the ________ of an atom is the ________. The mass of the proton is ________ atomic mass unit. The number of protons in the nucleus is the atom's atomic ________. All atoms of a given element have the same number of ________. The mass of a nucleus is ____________ the combined masses of the protons. The neutron is a particle found in the ________. This particle has ________ charge and has a mass about equal to the mass of one ________. The sum of the ________ and ________ in a nucleus is the mass number. In elements with 20 or fewer protons, the number of protons is about ________ the number of neutrons. In elements with more than 20 protons the number of protons is generally ________ than the number of neutrons.

Isotopes

Atoms with the same ________ number but different ________ numbers are isotopes of the same element. The nucleus of an isotope is called a(n) ________. When a sample of an element is analyzed in a mass ____________, there is ________ spot on the film for each isotope. All isotopes of an element have the same number of ________ around the nucleus, and have the same ________ behavior. The notation for isotopes involves a superscript and a subscript, both of which are written to the ________ of the ________ for the element. The ________ number is the subscript and the ________ number is the superscript.

Radioactive Decay

Nuclei that decay are described as ____________. Rutherford identified ________ kinds of radiation. Two of the forms, ________ and ________, are charged particles. Gamma radiation is made up of high-energy ________. The release of an alpha particle causes a nucleus to lose ________ charge units and ________ mass units. The element has been changed, or ____________, into a different element. Beta particles are high-speed ________, and have a(n) ________ charge. In beta decay, the ________ number increases by one and the ________ number does not change. Gamma radiation results from the redistribution of ________ in the nucleus. Gamma radiation does not change the ________ number or the ________ number.

CHAPTER 30 Study Guide

NAME ______________________________

Nuclear Reactions and Equations

A nuclear reaction occurs whenever the number of ________ or ________ in the nucleus changes. The emission of particles from a(n) __________ nucleus releases energy in the form of _______ energy of the emitted particles. The nuclear reaction does not destroy any ________. In a nuclear reaction, electric charge is __________.

Half-Life

The time required for ________ of the atoms in a sample of radioactive isotope to _______ is the half-life of that isotope. The number of decays per _______ is the activity of the substance. Activity is ___________ to the number of radioactive atoms present. The activity is reduced by ________ during one half-life of the sample.

NAME ______________________________

30.2 THE BUILDING BLOCKS OF MATTER

Nuclear Bombardment

Rutherford used ______ particles to cause nuclear reactions. As a result, high-speed ________ were released by nuclei. Because neutrons are __________, they are not repelled by a nucleus, which makes them useful in bombarding nuclei. One of the problems with using alpha particles is that they have ______ energies, and need to be artificially __________ to higher energies.

Linear Accelerators

A linear accelerator is a series of hollow ______ in a long __________ chamber. Protons are produced and accelerated into a tube that has a(n) ________ potential. Alternating charges produce _______ fields between tubes, which __________ the protons along the path. Both _______ and ________ can be accelerated in a linear accelerator.

The Synchrotron

A synchrotron uses ________ fields to move charged particles in _______ paths. In between the magnets, there are regions in which high-frequency alternating _______ accelerates the particles. In a synchrotron it is possible to send particles in two directions so that they will ______.

Particle Detectors

Photographic ______ becomes "fogged" when exposed to radiation. High-speed particles ionize matter, and remove ________ from atoms. Some substances ________ when exposed to radiation, and this light can be used to detect radiation. In a Geiger-Mueller tube, particles ionize ______ atoms. The positive particle is accelerated toward the cylinder with the ________ charge. The negative particle is accelerated toward the wire with the ________ charge. As the charged particles strike and ionize other particles they create a pulse of _______ in the tube. In a cloud chamber, particles leave a trail of ______ on which water vapor __________. A(n) ______ chamber is like a huge Geiger-Mueller tube. Because a(n) _______ particle does not produce a discharge, laws of conservation of _______ and __________ are used to see if these particles were part of any collisions.

The Fundamental Particles

The two families of particles of which matter is made are _______ and _______. Protons and neutrons are made up of _______. The electron is a(n) _______. Some additional particles transmit ______ between particles. The electromagnetic force is carried by the _______. The binding forces in the nuclei are carried by _______. The ___________ are involved in weak interaction, which operates in ______ decay. Although the particle that carries __________ force has not been detected, it is called the ________. Antiparticles are identical to particles except for having the ________ charge. When a particle and its antiparticle collide they ________ each other and are transformed into _______, or lighter

CHAPTER 30 Study Guide

NAME ______________________________

particle-antiparticle pairs and ________. The total number of quarks and leptons in the universe is ________. Quarks and leptons are ________ and __________ only in particle-antiparticle pairs.

Particles and Antiparticles

The energy released when a neutron decays is shared by the ____________ and ___________ that are produced. The antineutrino has ______ mass and no charge, but it carries ___________ and energy. Emission of a positron is similar to ______ decay. A proton changes into a(n) ________ and emits a positron and a(n) _________. When a positron and a(n) ________ collide, they annihilate each other, producing ________ rays. In this process, matter is converted into ________. Energy can be converted into _______ by a process called ______ production. If a gamma ray with enough energy passes close to a(n) ________, a positron and a(n) ________ are formed. If the gamma ray has more than the minimum amount of energy, the extra energy goes into the _______ energy of the positron and electron.

The Quark Model of Nucleons

The proton and the ________ are made up of quarks. A proton is made up of two ______ quarks and one ______ quark. A neutron is made up of one ______ quark and two ______ quarks. The force that holds quarks together becomes _________ as the quarks are pulled farther apart. Weak bosons are involved in ______ decay. In this process, one ______ quark in a neutron changes to a(n) ______ quark, and one ___________ is emitted. Then this boson decays into an electron and a(n) ___________. Bombardment of particles at high _________ creates particles with very ______ lifetimes. Such particles, made of ______________ pairs, are mesons. Particles made of ______ quarks are baryons. To account for all the different particles that can be produced in accelerators, a total of ______ quarks and ______ leptons are needed.

DATE ________ PERIOD ________ NAME ________________________

CHAPTER 31 Study Guide

Fill in the blanks as you study the chapter.

31.1 HOLDING THE NUCLEUS TOGETHER

The Strong Nuclear Force

The strong nuclear force overcomes the mutual repulsion between ________ in the nucleus. The force acts over a range about the size of the _______ of a proton. The strength of the strong force between two protons is ________ the strength of the strong force between a proton and a neutron. To remove a proton or a neutron from a nucleus, _______ must be done to overcome the attractive _______. Doing work increases the ________ of a system. This means that the assembled nucleus has _______ energy than the separate nucleons that make up the nucleus. The difference in energy is the ________ energy of the nucleus. Because the nucleus has less energy than its parts, the sign of the binding energy is ________.

Binding Energy of the Nucleus

The binding energy of a nucleus is proportional to the difference between the ______ of the nucleus and the ________ of the nucleons from which it is made. The difference between these two masses is the mass _______, which can be determined experimentally. From this value, the ________ energy can be calculated. For most nuclei, the binding energy per nucleon becomes more _________ as the ______ number increases to 56. This isotope of iron has the _______ tightly-bound nucleus. Nuclei that are smaller or larger are _______ tightly bound. A nuclear reaction will occur naturally if the reaction releases ________. This occurs if the new nucleus is _______ tightly bound than the original nucleus. When a heavy nucleus decays by the release of an alpha particle, the binding ________per nucleon of the new nucleus is _______ than that of the original nucleus. The excess energy is transferred into the _______ energy of the alpha particle. For small nuclei, reactions that _________ the number of nucleons in a nucleus make the binding energy more _________. Such a reaction occurs on the sun, where the excess energy becomes the _______________ radiation that we see as light.

CHAPTER 31 Study Guide

NAME ___

31.2 USING NUCLEAR ENERGY

Artificial Radioactivity

Radioactive isotopes can be formed from ___ isotopes if they are ___ with ___ rays or particles such as alpha particles or neutrons. The unstable nuclei that form emit ___ until they are ___ into stable isotopes. Artificially-produced isotopes, called ___, allow doctors to follow the path of molecules in the body. A PET scanner uses isotopes that emit ___. The scanner identifies ___ rays produced when a(n) ___ pair annihilate each other. A ___ then makes a three-dimensional map of the distribution of decaying ___. Radioactivity is also used as a way to destroy certain ___, as in cancer patients. Unstable particles produced in a particle ___ can also be used to kill cells.

Nuclear Fission

Nuclear fission is the splitting of a(n) ___ into two or ___ fragments of approximately ___ size. Such a reaction involves the release of a large amount of ___. Some isotopes of uranium undergo fission when they are bombarded with ___. To find the energy released by each fission, write a(n) ___ for the reaction and calculate the ___ on each side of the equation. The right side of the equation should show less ___ than the left side of the equation. This energy equivalent is transferred to the ___ energy of the fission products. Since fission reactions release ___, which can split other uranium atoms, the reaction continues, and is called a(n) ___ reaction.

Nuclear Reactors

Most of the neutrons produced in fission are moving at speeds that are too ___ to cause additional fissions. In a nuclear reactor, the ___ surrounds the uranium fuel and provides light atoms with which fast neutrons will ___. When a neutron collides with a light atom, it transfers ___ and energy to the atom. The neutron then becomes a(n) ___ neutron, which can split another uranium nucleus. Graphite and heavy water can be used as ___ in reactors that have as little as 1% $^{235}_{92}U$, which is the fissionable isotope. If ordinary water is to be used as a moderator, the amount of this isotope must be ___ by a process called ___. In the United States, most reactors are ___ reactors. In these reactors, water is both the ___ and the coolant, which transfers ___ energy away from the fissioning uranium. In the reactor, rods of a substance, such as cadmium, which can absorb ___ are used to regulate the rate of the ___ reaction. When these ___ rods are inserted all the way into the reactor, the chain reaction ___. The thermal energy that is released by fission heats water, which flows under ___ to a heat ___, where the thermal energy boils water in a separate circuit. The boiling water produces ___, which

NAME ______________________________

turns a(n) ________. After fission takes place, the fuel rods from the reactor contain ___________ waste products which must be removed and stored in a safe place. There is a limited amount of uranium, so scientists are working on the ________ reactor, which produces ______ nuclear fuel than it uses.

Nuclear Fusion

Fusion is the union of ______ nuclei to produce _______ ones. The larger nucleus is _______ tightly bound, so its mass is _______ than the masses of the smaller nuclei. The energy __________ of this mass is very large, and is transferred to the _______ energy of the particles that are formed. In the sun, fusion converts four ________ into one _______ nucleus. Because fusion requires huge amounts of ________ energy, these reactions are sometimes called _____________ reactions.

Controlled Fusion

To confine the fusion reaction in a controlled fusion, _________ fields are used to hold the ________, made up of electrons and ions. An increase in the magnetic field can _________ the temperature of the plasma, causing __________ nuclei to fuse into _______ nuclei. The energy released could be used to ______ some material which would then ______ water to turn a(n) ________. Currently, fusion reactions use _______ energy than they produce. Another way to control fusion is to enclose the fuel in tiny glass ________, and then direct ______ beams at them. The pellets then ________, which increases the pressure. The increased pressure increases the ___________ to levels needed for fusion to occur.

DATE ______ PERIOD ______ NAME ____________

CHAPTER 1 Study Guide

Fill in the blanks as you study the chapter.

Physics: The Search for Understanding

Physics is the branch of knowledge that studies the _physical_ world. Scientists who work in this field are known as _physicists_. They study the nature of _matter_ and _energy_, and how they are related. In their work, scientists try to find powerful _explanations_ that describe more than one phenomenon, and lead to a better understanding of the _universe_. A(n) _theory_ is a framework of explanations hypothesizing how a discovery works. Physicists use _mathematics_ and _computers_ in developing theories. A theory can _explain_ experimental data and _predict_ results to new experiments. It can be developed before or after the results of _experiments_ are seen. Physicists describe relationships, or _laws_, often using mathematics.

What and How, not Why: Scientific Methods

Aristotle and his followers made _observations_ of occurrences, and then used only _logical argument_ to draw conclusions. Galileo Galilei was one of the first European scientists to state that knowledge should be based on _observations_ and _experiments_. Following Galileo's method of _observation_, _experiment_, and _analysis_, scientists approach problems in a(n) _organized_ way. Although the approach to the problem can vary, any organized approach is referred to as the _scientific method_. The results of experiments are carefully _analyzed_ because conclusions are drawn. Conclusions are then _tested_ further to see if they are valid.

DATE ______ PERIOD ______ NAME ____________

CHAPTER 2 Study Guide

Fill in the blanks as you study the chapter.

2.1 THE MEASURE OF SCIENCE

The Metric System

In the metric system, units of different sizes are related by _powers of ten_. The initials _SI_ stand for the International System of Units. The three fundamental units measure the quantities _length_, _mass_, and _time_. The meter is the SI unit of _length_. The second is the SI unit of _time_. The kilogram is the SI unit of _mass_. Other units are called derived units because they are _combinations_ of fundamental units.

Scientific Notation

Scientific notation is based on _exponential_ notation. In scientific notation, a measurement is expressed as a number between _one_ and _ten_ multiplied by a whole-number _power_ of ten. When numbers are converted to scientific notation, the decimal point is moved until there is one _non-zero_ digit to the _left_ of the decimal point. The number of places the decimal point is moved is used as the _exponent_ of ten. If the decimal point is moved to the _left_, the exponent becomes larger. If the decimal point is moved to the _right_, the exponent becomes smaller.

Prefixes Used with SI Units

SI units are changed by powers of _ten_ by the use of prefixes. The prefix for one tenth is _deci-_. The prefix for one thousandth is _milli-_. The prefix that changes a unit by one thousand is _kilo-_. All metric units use _the same_ prefixes.

Arithmetic Operations in Scientific Notation

When numbers are in scientific notation, they may be added or subtracted if the numbers have the same _exponent_. After the numbers are added, the exponent is _the same_. If the powers of ten are not the same, the _decimal point_ must be moved, and the _exponent_ must be changed before the numbers can be added. For multiplying numbers in scientific notation, the _exponents_ do not have to be the same. After the numbers are multiplied, the exponents are _added_ and the units are _multiplied_.

CHAPTER 2 Study Guide

NAME ______________________

2.2 NOT ALL IS CERTAIN

Uncertainties of Measurements

A common source of error in making measurements comes from the **angle** at which the instrument is read. Parallax is the apparent change in **position** of an object when it is seen from different **angles**. Reading instruments at **eye** level and **straight on** reduces error due to parallax.

Accuracy and Precision

Precision is the degree of **exactness** to which the measurement of a quantity can be **reproduced**. The precision of a measuring device is determined by the **finest** division on its scale. Accuracy is the extent to which a measured value agrees with the **standard** value of a quantity. Accuracy can be affected by changes in the **instrument** used to make the measurement. Uncertainties in measurement affect **accuracy** but not **precision**.

Significant Digits

In making measurements, there is a limit to the number of **digits** that are valid. This limitation is caused by the **precision** of the instrument used. The digits that are valid are called **significant** digits. The last significant digit in a measurement is a(n) **estimate**, so it is **uncertain**. All **non-zero** digits are considered to be significant. All final zeros **after** the decimal point are significant. Zeroes between two other significant digits **are** significant. Zeros used for spacing between significant digits and the decimal point **are not** significant.

Operations Using Significant Digits

The result of a mathematical operation with measurements cannot be more precise than the **least** precise measurement. When numbers are added or subtracted, the operation is performed first, and the answer is rounded off to correspond to the **least precise** value involved. When numbers are multiplied or divided, the operation is performed first, and then the answer is rounded off to **the same** number of significant digits as the factor with the **least** number of significant digits. Significant digits are used when calculating with **measurements**, but not when **counting**.

CHAPTER 2 Study Guide

NAME ______________________

2.3 DISPLAYING DATA

Graphing Data

When data are analyzed, the variable that is **manipulated** is the independent variable. The dependent variables are the **result** of the independent variable. The **independent** variable is plotted on the horizontal axis and the **dependent** variable is plotted on the vertical axis. After the dependent and independent variables have been identified, the **range** of each variable must be determined. It must be determined if the **origin** is a valid data point. Each axis should be **numbered** and **labeled**. Then the **data** are plotted and the **curve** is drawn. Finally, the graph should be given a(n) **title**.

Linear, Quadratic, and Inverse Relationships

The graph of a linear relationship is a(n) **straight line**. The equation for such a relationship is **$y = mx + b$**. In this equation, m represents the **slope** and b represents the **y-intercept**. When one variable varies directly with the square of the other, the curve is in the shape of a(n) **parabola**. The equation for such a curve is called a(n) **quadratic** equation, and is written as **$y = kx^2$**. In this equation, k represents a(n) **constant**. In an inverse relationship, the curve is a(n) **hyperbola**, and the equation that represents it is **$y = kx^{-1}$**.

CHAPTER 2 Study Guide

NAME ______________________________

2.4 MANIPULATING EQUATIONS

Solving Equations Using Algebra

In manipulating equations, the relationship must not be __changed__. If one side of the equation is divided by a variable, the other side of the equation should be __divided__ by that variable. Any operation performed on one side of the equation must be __the same as__ the operation performed on the other side of the equation. If the equation for density, $D = m/V$, is solved for m, the correct equation is __$m = DV$__.

Units in Equations

Before mathematical operations are carried out, all terms in the equation must have __the same__ units. When an answer is written, it must include both the numerical __value__ and the __unit__. If a term has several units, they are treated like any other mathematical __quantity__.

DATE __________ PERIOD __________ NAME ______________________________

CHAPTER 3 Study Guide

Fill in the blanks as you study the chapter.

3.1 HOW FAR AND HOW FAST?

Position and Distance

An object's __position__ can be described in terms of its relationship to a reference point. Choosing a reference point establishes a(n) __frame of__ reference. Describing distance does not need a(n) __frame of__ reference. Distance involves only a measurement of __length__, and is a(n) __scalar__ quantity. Position involves both __distance__ and __direction__, and is a(n) __vector__ quantity.

Average Velocity

If an object is moving, its position at one and only one time is a(n) __instantaneous__ position. The change in __position__ of an object is its displacement, which is a(n) __vector__ quantity. The average velocity of an object is the change in __distance__ divided by the __time interval__ over which the change occurred. Average velocity is calculated using the equation $\bar{v} = \frac{\Delta d}{\Delta t}$. In this equation, __$\Delta d$__, which is read as "delta d," stands for __displacement__. The symbol __Δt__, which is read as "delta t," stands for __time interval__. Average velocity is expressed in a unit made up of a(n) __length__ unit divided by a(n) __time__ unit. Different units used to describe average velocity can be changed from one to another by the use of __conversion__ factors.

Finding Displacement from Velocity and Time

Displacement can be calculated by using the equation __$\Delta d = \bar{v}\Delta t$__. In this equation, __$\bar{v}$__ represents average velocity and __Δt__ represents the time interval. If the average velocity of an object is the same at all __time intervals__, the object is described as moving at constant, or __uniform__, velocity. Constant velocity can be calculated using the equation $v = \frac{d}{t}$.

Position-Time Graphs

A position-time graph is used to show how __position__ depends on __time__. If the motion is constant, the data produce a(n) __straight__ line, which means that the relationship between time and position is __linear__.

The Slope of a Position-Time Graph

On a position-time graph, the displacement is the __vertical__ separation of two points. The time interval is the __horizontal__ separation. The slope of the line is the ratio of the __rise__ to the __run__. The __rise__ of the line represents displacement. The __run__ of the line represents the time interval. The slope of the line represents the __velocity__ of the object.

CHAPTER 3 Study Guide

NAME ______

3.2 NEW MEANINGS FOR OLD WORDS

Positive and Negative Velocities

Displacements can be __positive__ or __negative__, but time intervals are always __positive__. Displacements to the __right__ of the reference point are positive. Displacements to the __left__ of the reference point are negative. Speed is the __magnitude__ of velocity. Speed is generally shown as positive, but velocity can be __positive__ or __negative__.

Instantaneous Velocity

If motion is not constant, the position-time graph does not produce a(n) __straight__ line. A straight line can be drawn __tangent__ to the curve at any one point. The __slope__ of this line is the instantaneous velocity at that point.

Velocity-Time Graphs

In a velocity-time graph, __time__ is shown on the horizontal axis and __velocity__ is shown on the vertical axis. If velocity is constant, the velocity-time graph produces a(n) __straight__ line that is __parallel__ to the horizontal axis. If velocity is increasing, the line has a(n) __positive__ slope. If velocity is decreasing, the line has a(n) __negative__ slope. The __vertical__ value of any point on the line is the instantaneous velocity at that time. The area under the line on a velocity-time graph is equal to the __displacement__ of the object from its original __position__ to its __position__ at a given time.

Relativity of Velocity

Measurements of __position__ or __velocity__ depend on the observer's frame of reference. If a person walks slowly toward the back of a moving train, an observer on the train would say that velocity and displacement are __negative__. An observer standing on the station platform would say that the walker's velocity and displacement are __positive__. However, when velocities approach the __speed of light__, the frame of reference does not matter, and the velocity is __the same__. This concept is part of __Einstein's__ theory of relativity.

DATE ______ PERIOD ______ NAME ______

CHAPTER 4 Study Guide

Fill in the blanks as you study the chapter.

4.1 WHAT IS ACCELERATION?

Average Acceleration

The change in __velocity__ divided by the __time interval__ is average acceleration. It can be calculated using the equation $\bar{a} = \frac{\Delta v}{\Delta t}$. In this equation, __$\bar{a}$__ stands for acceleration, __Δv__ stands for change in velocity, and __Δt__ stands for the time interval. If velocity is measured in meters per second, acceleration is measured in __m/s/s__, which is read as __meters per second per second__. The unit also can be written as m/s^2, which is read as __meters per second squared__. Like velocity, acceleration is a(n) __vector__ quantity, which means it has both __magnitude__ and __direction__. When velocity __increases__, acceleration is positive. When velocity __decreases__, acceleration is negative.

Average and Instantaneous Acceleration

A velocity-time graph shows how __velocity__ depends on __time__. The rise of the curve represents the change in __velocity__. The run of the curve represents the __time interval__. The slope of the curve represents the __average acceleration__. If the curve on a velocity-time graph is a straight line, the acceleration is __constant__. If the curve is not a straight line, acceleration is __changing__. The slope of a line tangent to the curve is the __instantaneous acceleration__ at that time.

Velocity of an Object with Constant Acceleration

Acceleration that does not __change__ in time is constant, or __uniform__, acceleration. The velocity when the clock time is __zero__ is the initial velocity. The velocity after acceleration has occurred is called the __final__ velocity, and is calculated using the equation __$v_f = v_i + at$__. In this equation, v_f is __final velocity__, v_i is __initial velocity__, a is __acceleration__, and t is __time interval__.

CHAPTER 4 Study Guide

NAME ____________

4.2 DISPLACEMENT DURING CONSTANT ACCELERATION

Displacement When Velocity and Time Are Known

If an object is accelerating, its displacement can be calculated using the equation $d = \frac{1}{2}(v_f + v_i)t$ In this equation, __d__ stands for displacement, __v_f__ stands for final velocity, __v_i__ stands for initial velocity, and __t__ stands for time interval. To find displacement using a __velocity-time__ graph, find the area under the curve.

Displacement When Acceleration and Time Are Known

If initial velocity, acceleration, and time are known, the displacement of the object can be calculated using the equation $d = v_it + \frac{1}{2}at^2$. In this equation, v_it stands for the __displacement__ of the object if it were moving at __constant__ velocity. In the equation, the term $\frac{1}{2}at^2$ stands for the __displacement__ of the object starting from rest and moving with uniform __acceleration__. For an object accelerated from rest at a constant rate, the velocity-time graph produces a curve that is a(n) __straight line__, and the position-time graph produces a curve that is a(n) __half a parabola__. If a line is drawn tangent to the curve of the position-time graph, the slope of that line is the __instantaneous velocity__ at that point.

Displacement When Velocity and Acceleration Are Known

If initial and final velocities, as well as acceleration, are known, displacement can be calculated without using __time__. The equation for this calculation is $d = \frac{v_f^2 - v_i^2}{2a}$. In this equation, d stands for __displacement__, v_f stands for __finial velocity__, v_i stands for __initial velocity__, and a stands for __acceleration__.

Acceleration Due to Gravity

__Galileo__ was the first to show that all objects fall toward Earth with constant __acceleration__. The __mass__ of the object does not matter, as long as __air resistance__ can be ignored. Acceleration due to gravity is represented by the symbol __g__ . For an object falling downward, both __velocity__ and __acceleration__ are negative. Acceleration due to gravity is equal to __−9.80 m/s²__. As long as air resistance is ignored, the equations used involving acceleration can be used for falling objects if __a__ is replaced by g. Because there are so many equations that can be used, it is important to read each problem carefully, and then identify the quantities that are __given__ and the quantity that is __unknown__. After an equation is selected, it may have to be __rewritten__ before the known values can be __substituted__ in the equation.

DATE ________ PERIOD ________ NAME ____________

CHAPTER 5 Study Guide

Fill in the blanks as you study the chapter.

5.1 NEWTON'S LAWS OF MOTION

Forces

A force is a __push__ or a __pull__. Because a force is a vector quantity, it has both magnitude and __direction__. Physicists group all forces into four kinds. They are __gravitational force__, __electromagnetic force__, __strong nuclear force__, and __weak force__. The weakest of the four forces is __gravitational force__. Charged particles cause the __electromagnetic__ force to be exerted. The __strong nuclear__ force is the strongest of the four forces, but only acts over small distances. The __weak__ force is involved in the radioactive decay of some nuclei. This force has been linked with the __electromagnetic__ force.

Newton's First Law of Motion

Forces acting on an object can be __combined__ to produce the net force on the object. If all the forces acting in one direction are __equal to__ all the forces acting on the object in the opposite direction, the net force is zero. According to __Newton's first__ law, if there is no net force on an object, the object remains at rest, or moves with __constant__ velocity in a __straight__ line.

Newton's Second Law of Motion

If there is a net force on an object, the object will be accelerated, or change __velocity__. The amount of acceleration caused depends on the __size__ of the force and the __mass__ of the object. Newton's second law can be written as an equation, __$F = ma$__. This equation means that acceleration is __directly__ proportional to force and __inversely__ proportional to mass. The direction of the force and the direction of the acceleration are __the same__.

The Unit of Force

The unit of force is defined in terms of Newton's __second__ law. The unit of force is the __newton__, abbreviated as __N__. The amount of force that causes a mass of __one kilogram__ to accelerate at a rate of __one meter per second squared__ is equal to one newton.

Newton's Third Law of Motion

Newton's third law describes pairs of forces called __action-reaction__ forces. These two forces are __equal__ in magnitude and __opposite__ in direction. According to this law, if a book pushes downward on a table, the table pushes __upward__ against __the book__.

CHAPTER 5 Study Guide   NAME ____________

5.2 USING NEWTON'S LAW

Mass and Weight

An object's weight is the gravitational force acting on the object. The unit used to express measurements of weight is the newton. Newton's second law can be used to find the weight of an object. The acceleration caused by gravity is equal to 9.80 m/s^2, and is represented by the symbol g. The equation used for calculating weight is $F = mg$. According to the equation, an object's weight is proportional to its mass. An object's weight may vary from one location to another, because acceleration due to gravity may change from one place to another. However, the object's mass does not change.

Two Kinds of Mass

One way to determine mass is to measure the amount of force needed to accelerate the object. This is called inertial mass. The other way to determine mass is to use a balance to compare the effects of gravitational force on two objects. This is called gravitational mass. In experiments, these two determinations of mass have been shown to be equal.

Friction

If you push on an object and slide it across a surface, the force of friction will oppose the motion. Friction acts in a direction that is parallel to the surface on which the object slides, and opposite to the direction in which the object slides. Static friction opposes the start of an object's motion, and sliding friction opposes continuing the motion when the object is already in motion. Of these two forces, static friction is greater. The amount of friction can be calculated using the equation $F_f = \mu F_N$. The constant in the equation is called the coefficient of friction.

The Net Force Causes Acceleration

If more than one force acts on an object, the amount of acceleration can be calculated using Newton's second law. However, before the equation in Newton's law is used, the net force, which is the sum of the forces, must be found. The positive and negative signs on the forces are important because they indicate the direction of the forces.

The Fall of Bodies in the Air

Without any air, all objects fall with the same acceleration. When air is present, a friction-like force, called the drag force, acts on the object. This force depends on the size and shape of the object, the density of the air, and the speed of motion. When this force is equal to the force of gravity, the net force on the object is zero, and the object has reached its terminal velocity.

DATE ________ PERIOD ________ NAME ____________

CHAPTER 6 Study Guide

Fill in the blanks as you study the chapter.

6.1 GRAPHICAL METHOD OF VECTOR ADDITION

Vector Addition in One Dimension

An arrow-tipped line segment is used to represent a vector. To add two vectors, place the tail of one vector at the head of the other vector, as shown below. The diagram represents an airplane flying east at 125 km/h. There is a 25.0-km/h tail wind. The long vector represents the velocity of the airplane. The short vector represents the velocity of the wind. When adding these two vectors, the order of addition does not matter. However, the direction and the length of each vector must not be changed when drawn.

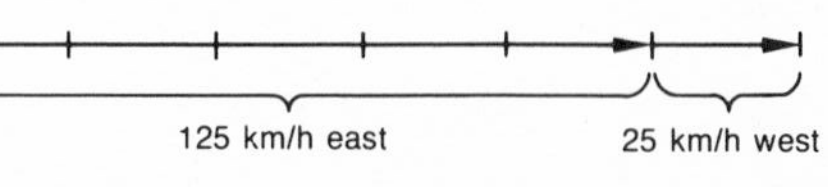

Vector Addition in Two Dimensions

When vectors in two dimensions are added, the tail of one vector is placed at the head of the other vector, as shown below. The diagram represents an airplane flying east at 125 km/h. There is a 25.0-km/h cross wind blowing north. The long vector represents the velocity of the airplane. The short vector represents the velocity of the wind. The resultant vector is drawn from the tail of the first vector to the head of the second vector. The direction of the resultant is expressed as an angle measured counterclockwise from the east.

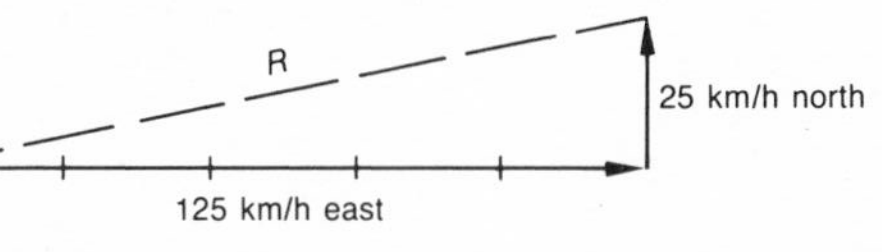

Addition of Several Vectors

When more than two vectors are added, the order in which they are added is not important. However, the length and direction of each vector are important, and must not be changed. The diagram should show one vector for each force or motion involved.

Independence of Vector Quantities

The path of an airplane in a cross wind is determined by the airplane's own velocity and that of the wind. If the cross wind increases to 30.0 km/h, the wind vector and the resultant vector are changed, but the airplane vector is not changed.

6.2 ANALYTICAL METHOD OF VECTOR ADDITION

Adding Perpendicular Vectors

When two vectors are perpendicular, the vector diagram produces a right triangle, in which the resultant vector is the hypotenuse of the triangle. In the diagram below, an airplane flying east at 125 km/h is affected by a 25.0-km/h cross wind blowing to the north. The Pythagorean theorem can be used to calculate the length of the resultant vector. The equation to be used is $R^2 = a^2 + b^2$. The resultant is equal to 127 km/h. Trigonometry can be used to calculate the direction the resultant. The equation used is $\tan \theta = \frac{\text{side opposite}}{\text{side adjacent}}$, and the direction of the resultant is 12° north of east.

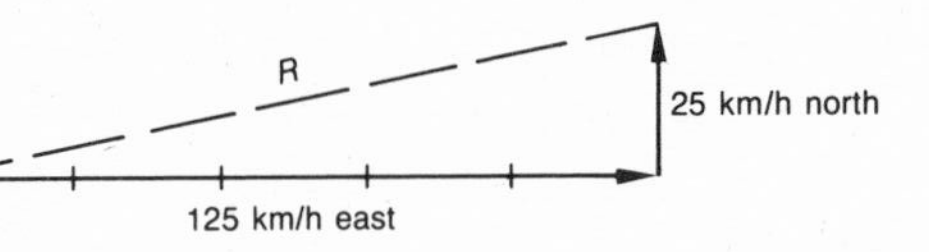

Components of Vectors

Any single vector can be thought of as a(n) resultant of two vectors, called components. Usually the components are chosen to be perpendicular, so that trigonometry can be used to determine the size of each component. The diagram below shows the path of a football player running 25 m at an angle of 14° with the sideline. Complete the diagram by drawing the two component vectors, using the sideline as the component representing the player's forward progress. The magnitude of this component can be calculated using the cosine of 14°. The sideways component of the player's path can be calculated using the sine of 14°. This process of finding components of a single vector is called vector resolution.

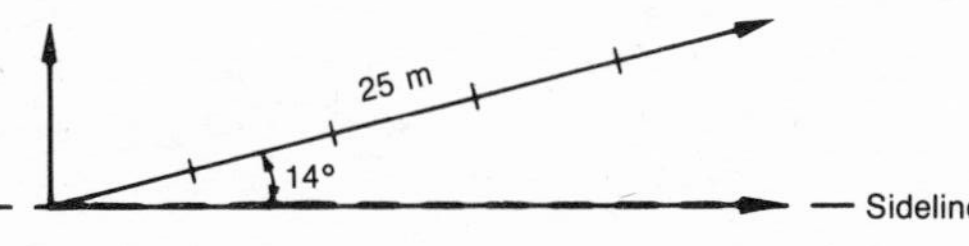

Adding Vectors at Any Angle

Vector resolution is used when adding vectors that are not perpendicular. Each vector is resolved into two components. When three vectors are added, vector resolution produces a total of six components. Of these components, three are in the horizontal direction and can be added together. The remaining three components are in the vertical direction and can be added together. After adding these components, there is only one horizontal vector and one vertical vector. Finally, the resultant vector is found using the Pythagorean theorem.

6.3 APPLICATIONS OF VECTORS

Equilibrium

An object is in equilibrium when the net sum, or resultant, of all forces acting on it is zero. The object will not be accelerated. If the sum is not zero, adding another vector will make the sum zero. The force that is represented by this added vector is called the equilibrant force. This added force is equal in magnitude to the resultant of the other forces, and opposite in direction to the resultant.

Gravitational Force and Inclined Planes

The weight of an object is caused by gravitational force acting on an object in a downward direction. When an object rests on an inclined plane, this force can be resolved into two components that are perpendicular to each other. One component is perpendicular to the surface of the inclined plane, and is equal to the force exerted by the object on the inclined plane. The other component is parallel to the surface of the inclined plane. This is the force that causes the object to be accelerated down the inclined plane. As the inclined plane becomes steeper, this component increases in magnitude, and acceleration increases. However, acceleration will not occur until this force overcomes friction between the object and the inclined plane. The amount of friction depends on the component force that is perpendicular to the surface of the inclined plane. The amount of friction also depends on the coefficient of friction.

DATE ________ PERIOD ________ NAME ____________________

CHAPTER 7 Study Guide

Fill in the blanks as you study the chapter.

7.1 PROJECTILE MOTION

Independence of Motion in Two Dimensions

The path a projectile follows is called its __trajectory__. An object that is thrown has a(n) __constant__ horizontal velocity. An object that is dropped has a(n) __constant__ horizontal velocity that is equal to __zero__. In both cases, there is no horizontal force acting on the projectile after it is released, so there is no horizontal __acceleration__. Both a thrown object and a dropped object are accelerated downward by the __force of gravity__. The amount of acceleration of the thrown object is __equal to__ the amount of acceleration of the dropped object. A projectile launched from a moving source will have different trajectories when seen by observers with different __frames of reference__. An observer moving with the source of the projectile will see the trajectory as having no __horizontal__ component. However, an observer not moving with the source of the projectile will see the trajectory as having both a(n) __horizontal__ and a(n) __vertical__ component. The frame of reference affects how one sees the projectile's __trajectory__ and __horizontal__ motion, but not its __vertical__ motion.

Objects Launched Horizontally

If a projectile is launched horizontally, its initial horizontal velocity may vary, but the initial vertical velocity is __zero__. The vertical acceleration is __$-9.80\ m/s^2$__. The horizontal acceleration is __zero__. As the projectile follows its trajectory, its vertical velocity __increases__ while its horizontal velocity __stays the same__.

Objects Launched at an Angle

If an object is bouncing, its vertical velocity is __positive__ as the object bounces up. Vertical velocity is __zero__ at the top of the path. Vertical velocity is __negative__ as the object falls downward. When the object returns to the launch position, the vertical speed is __the same__ as it was at the launch and its direction is __reversed__. The range is the __horizontal__ distance travelled by the bouncing object. In solving projectile motion problems, the initial velocity should be resolved into its __horizontal__ and __vertical__ components. If the launching and landing positions are at equal heights, the rising and falling times are __equal__. The horizontal distance moved in the first half of the trajectory is __equal to__ the horizontal distance moved in the second half of the trajectory.

CHAPTER 7 Study Guide NAME ____________________

7.2 PERIODIC MOTION

Circular Motion

If an object is moving with uniform circular motion, the speed is __constant__. Velocity is __changing__ because the direction is __changing__. In uniform circular motion, the radius of the path is __constant__. The velocity is __perpendicular__ to the radius and __tangent__ to the circular path. Any vector that is tangent to the circle represents the __instantaneous velocity__ at that point. All such vectors will have the same __length__, but different __directions__. The vector that represents acceleration is in the direction of the __radius__, pointing toward the __center__ of the circle. __Centripetal__ acceleration points toward the center of the circle. It is __directly__ proportional to the square of the speed and __inversely__ proportional to the radius of the circle. According to Newton's __second__ law, centripetal acceleration must be caused by a(n) __force__ that acts toward the center of the circle. The force that causes centripetal acceleration is called __centripetal force__. If this force disappears, the object in uniform circular motion will travel on a path that is a(n) __straight__ line __tangent__ to the circle.

Changing Circular Motion: Torque

To start or stop circular motion, the force applied to the object must have a component that is __parallel__ to the object's velocity. The product of the __force__ and the __lever arm__ is called torque. The greater the torque, the __greater__ the change in rotational motion.

Simple Harmonic Motion

When a vibrating object is moved away from its __equilibrium__ position, a force in the system pulls the object back to the __equilibrium__ position. Such a force is called a(n) __restoring force__. If this force varies linearly with the object's __displacement__, the motion is described as simple harmonic motion. In simple harmonic motion, the __period__ is the time needed to repeat one cycle of motion. The amplitude is the maximum __displacement__ the object moves from the __equilibrium position__. When a spring is stretched, the amount of restoring force exerted by the spring __increases__ linearly with the amount of force applied to the spring. This relationship is known as __Hooke's law__. When a spring is stretched by the weight of an object attached to it, the period of the spring's motion depends on the __mass of the object__ and the __stiffness of the spring__. The period does not depend on the __amplitude__. For a pendulum, the period depends on the __length__ of the pendulum. It does not depend on the __mass__ or the __amplitude__ of the pendulum. The __amplitude__ of a vibrating object can be increased by applying __external__ forces at regular __time intervals__, producing an effect called __mechanical resonance__. The time interval between the applied __forces__ must equal the __period__ of the vibrating object.

DATE ______ PERIOD ______ NAME ______________________

CHAPTER 8 Study Guide

Fill in the blanks as you study the chapter.

8.1 MOTION IN THE HEAVENS AND ON EARTH

Kepler's Laws of Planetary Motion

Tycho Brahe studied the motion of the planets in order to be able to __predict__ astronomical events. He believed that __Earth__ was the center of the universe. Johannes Kepler believed that __the sun__ was the center of the universe. He analyzed Brahe's data, and developed __three__ laws of planetary motion. One law says that the paths of the planets are __ellipses__ with __the sun__ located at one focus. Another law states that an imaginary line extending from the sun to a planet will sweep out equal __areas__ in equal amounts of time. According to this law, planets move __fastest__ when closest to the sun and move __slowest__ when farthest from the sun. Kepler's last law states that the ratio of the squares of the __periods__ of any two planets in orbit around the sun is equal to the ratio of the __cubes__ of their distances from __the sun__. This law can be stated as an equation, $\left(\frac{T_a}{T_b}\right)^2 = \left(\frac{r_a}{r_b}\right)^3$. To use this law to calculate the period of a satellite, you must know the __radius__ of its orbit and the __period__ and __radius__ of the orbit of another satellite.

Universal Gravitation

Newton showed that if the path of a planet were an ellipse, then the net force on the planet varies __inversely__ with the __square__ of the distance between the planet and the sun. Newton's law of universal gravitation can be stated in an equation, $F = G\frac{m_1m_2}{d^2}$. In this equation, F stands for __force__ and __d__ is the distance between the centers of the masses. G is a __constant__. According to this law, if the mass of one of the objects is doubled, the force of attraction is __doubled__. If the mass of one of the objects is halved, the force of attraction is __halved__. If the distance between the centers of the masses is doubled, the force is decreased to __one-fourth__.

Newton's Use of His Law of Universal Gravitation

Newton combined his law of universal gravitation with his __second__ law of motion. Using these two laws, he was able to derive the equation for __Kepler's__ third law.

Weighing Earth

The value of G was first calculated by __Henry Cavendish__. He measured the force of __attraction__ between two masses, and used Newton's __law of universal gravitation__ to calculate G. G is equal to __6.67×10^{-11} N•m²/kg²__.

CHAPTER 8 Study Guide

NAME ______________________

8.2 USING THE LAW OF UNIVERSAL GRAVITATION

Motion of Planets and Satellites

The motion of a projectile follows a(n) __parabolic__ trajectory. This path has both a(n) __vertical__ component and a(n) __horizontal__ component. If the velocity of the __horizontal__ component is great enough, the path of the projectile will follow a curve that matches the curve of __Earth__, and the projectile will be in __orbit__. A satellite in an orbit that is always the same height above Earth is said to move with __uniform circular motion__.

Weight and Weightlessness

The __acceleration__ of objects due to Earth's gravitation can be calculated using the __inverse__ square law and Newton's __second__ law of motion. These calculations show that as the distance from Earth increases, the acceleration due to Earth's gravity __decreases__. A satellite in orbit is subject to this acceleration, and it is in a condition known as __freefall__. The downward force of gravity is unbalanced and there is no __upward__ force acting on a satellite in orbit. Because of the unbalanced force, the satellite and everything in it seem to be __weightless__.

The Gravitational Field

Anything that has mass is surrounded by a __gravitational field__. The strength of this field is equal to the acceleration of __gravity__. The strength of the field varies __inversely__ with the __square__ of the distance from the center of Earth.

Einstein's Theory of Gravity

According to Albert Einstein, gravity is not a __force__, but is an effect of __space__. An object that has mass causes space to be __curved__. When other objects move in this space, they are __accelerated__ as they move along a curve. Einstein's theory is called the general theory of __relativity__. This theory explains why the path of light can be deflected when it passes the __sun__. This theory also explains that no light escapes from a(n) __black hole__ because the light is completely turned around by the huge amount of __mass__.

DATE ________ PERIOD ________ NAME ____________________

CHAPTER 9 Study Guide

Fill in the blanks as you study the chapter.

9.1 IMPULSE AND CHANGE IN MOMENTUM

Momentum and Impulse

The amount of force needed to change the motion of a moving object depends on the __velocity__ and __mass__ of the object. The momentum of a body is the product of the body's __mass__ and __velocity__. Momentum is a(n) __vector__ quantity. Its direction is __the same as__ the direction of the velocity. The equation used to calculate momentum is __$p = mv$__. In this equation, p stands for __momentum__, m stands for __mass__, and v stands for __velocity__. The unit for momentum is the __kilogram•meter/second__. The product of the __force__ applied to an object and the __time interval__ over which it acts is called the impulse. The direction of the impulse is __the same as__ the direction of the force that is applied. The unit for impulse is the __newton•second__. The impulse given to an object is equal to the change in the object's __momentum__. This equality is the __impulse-momentum__ theorem. It is also another statement of Newton's __second__ law of motion.

Angular Momentum

If a(n) __torque__ is applied to an object moving in a circle, the speed of the object changes. The quantity of angular motion that is similar to linear __momentum__ is called angular momentum. To calculate the angular momentum of a body, the body's __mass__, __velocity__, and __distance__ from the center of rotation must be known. The angular momentum of a planet in orbit is __constant__, although the distance from the sun varies. The planet's __velocity__ also varies, and is greatest when the planet is __nearest to__ the sun.

CHAPTER 9 Study Guide NAME ____________________

9.2 THE CONSERVATION OF MOMENTUM

Newton's Third Law and Momentum

If one object collides with another, the momentum of each object __changes__. The first object exerts a(n) __force__ on the second object, and the second object exerts a(n) __force__ of __equal__ magnitude and __opposite__ direction on the first object. If objects neither leave nor enter a system, the system is described as __closed__. If no external forces act on a system, the system is described as __isolated__. When there is a collision within such a system, the net change in momentum is __zero__. The total momentum before the collision is __equal to__ the total momentum after the collision.

Law of Conservation of Momentum

In a closed, isolated system, the momentum __does not change__. This statement is the law of __conservation of momentum__. When two objects within the system collide, the magnitude of the momentum lost by one of the objects is __equal to__ the momentum gained by the other object. Momentum can be __transferred__ from one object in the __system__ to another.

Internal and External Forces

Internal forces act between objects in __the same__ system. External forces are exerted by objects __outside__ the system. The total momentum of a system is conserved only when there are no __external__ forces acting on the system.

Conservation of Momentum in Two Dimensions

The law of conservation of momentum does not depend on the __directions__ in which objects move before and after colliding. The momentum of two objects in a system can be represented by two __vectors__, which can be resolved into vertical and horizontal __components__. After all vectors are added, the final sum must equal the __original__ momentum of the system.

DATE ______ PERIOD ______ NAME ______________________

CHAPTER 10 Study Guide

Fill in the blanks as you study the chapter.

10.1 WORK AND ENERGY

Work

Work is the product of the force exerted on an object and the distance the object moves in the direction of the force. The equation used to calculate work is $W = Fd$. In this equation, W stands for work, F stands for force, and d stands for distance. Work has no direction, so it is a scalar quantity. The SI unit of work is the joule. When a force of one newton moves an object a distance of one meter, one joule of work is done. Work is done on an object only if the object moves. Work is done only if the force and the displacement are in the same direction.

Work and Direction of Force

If a force is exerted in the direction of the motion, work is done. If a force is exerted perpendicular to the motion, no work is done. If a force is exerted at another angle to the motion, only the component of the force in the direction of the motion does work. The magnitude of this component is found by multiplying the force applied by the cosine of the angle between the force and the direction of the motion. When friction opposes motion, the work done by friction is negative. When work is done on an object, energy is transferred. Work is the transfer of energy as the result of motion. This transfer can be positive or negative.

Power

Power is the rate of doing work, or the rate at which energy is transferred. The equation used to calculate power is $P = \frac{W}{t}$. In this equation, P stands for power, W stands for work, and t stands for time. The unit of power is the watt. One joule of energy transferred in one second equals one watt. This is a very small unit, so power is often measured in kilowatts.

CHAPTER 10 Study Guide NAME ______________________

10.2 MACHINES

Simple and Complex Machines

A machine eases the load by changing the magnitude or direction of a force. A machine does not change the amount of work that is done. When a machine is used, the work that is done to the machine is called the input work. The work that the machine does is the output work. The machine transfers energy, but is not a source of energy. The machine's output work cannot be larger than the input work.

Energy Conservation and Mechanical Advantage

The force that is exerted on a machine is the effort force. The force exerted by a machine is the resistance force. The ratio of these forces is the mechanical advantage of the machine. The equation used to calculate mechanical advantage is $MA = \frac{F_r}{F_e}$. When the mechanical advantage is greater than one, the machine increases the force that is applied. If a machine transfers all of the energy, the output work equals the input work. The distances moved can be used to calculate the ideal mechanical advantage, using the equation $IMA = \frac{d_e}{D_r}$. The efficiency of a machine is the ratio of the output work to the input work. An ideal machine has an efficiency of 100%. A real machine has an efficiency of less than 100%. The lower the efficiency, the greater the effort force needed to produce the same resistance force. The lever, pulley, and inclined planes are examples of simple machines.

Compound Machines

A compound machine is made up of two or more simple machines, which are linked so that the resistance force of one machine becomes the effort force of the next machine. The mechanical advantage of a compound machine is the product of the mechanical advantages of the simple machines of which it is made.

The Human Walking Machine

Many body structures are levers, which are simple machines. In these human systems, a bone forms a(n) rigid bar and muscle contractions are a source of force. The movable joints between bones form a(n) fulcrum. The resistance is the weight of the body or any object being moved by the body. The mechanical advantages of these systems are low, and use a large amount of energy.

DATE ______ PERIOD ______ NAME ______________________

CHAPTER 11 Study Guide

Fill in the blanks as you study the chapter.

11.1 ENERGY IN ITS MANY FORMS

Forms of Energy

A moving object is able to change __itself__ and its __environment__. Moving objects have __kinetic__ energy. This energy comes from stored energy that is called __potential__ energy. Energy is transferred to an object when __work__ is done on the object. The amount of potential energy an object has depends on the object's __position__, __shape__, or __form__.

Doing Work to Change Kinetic Energy

An object's kinetic energy is proportional to the __mass__ of the object. Kinetic energy is also proportional to the square of the __velocity__. The equation used to calculate kinetic energy is $KE = \frac{1}{2}mv^2$. The unit used to measure kinetic energy is the __joule__. Increasing the amount of work done on an object __increases__ the amount of kinetic energy the object receives. According to the work-energy theorem, the __net work__ done on an object is equal to its __change__ in kinetic and potential energy. The net work done on an object is positive if the net force acts in the __same__ direction as the motion. If net work is positive, the object's kinetic energy __increases__. The net work done is negative if the net force acts in the __opposite__ direction to the motion. If the net work is negative, the object's kinetic energy __decreases__.

Potential Energy

In a moving object, kinetic energy can be changed to __potential__ energy and then to __kinetic__ energy. The total energy of the object is the sum of its __potential energy__ and __kinetic energy__. When a ball is thrown in the air, all of its energy is __kinetic__ energy at the start of its flight. This energy is changed into __potential__ energy. When the ball reaches its highest point, its speed is __zero__. At this point, it has no __kinetic__ energy, only __potential__ energy. As the ball falls downward, its speed __increases__ and __potential__ energy is changed to __kinetic__ energy. The equation used to calculate potential energy is $PE = mgh$. In this equation, h stands for __height__, which is measured against another position, called the __reference level__. This formula is only valid if acceleration is __constant__.

NAME ______________________

CHAPTER 11 Study Guide

11.2 CONSERVATION OF ENERGY

Systems

In a closed, isolated system, objects do not __enter__ or __leave__, and no __external__ forces act on the system. Under these conditions, the law of __conservation of energy__ states that energy can change __form__, but the total amount of energy is __constant__. According to this law, energy cannot be __created__ or __destroyed__. In a closed, isolated system, the sum of the potential and kinetic energy of an object can be called the __mechanical__ energy. If there is an increase in an object's kinetic energy, there will be a(n) __decrease__ in its potential energy. The __simple harmonic__ motion of a pendulum can show the law of conservation of energy. When the pendulum bob is raised to start the motion, it is given __potential__ energy. As the bob moves downward, the amount of __kinetic__ energy increases. At the lowest point of the pendulum bob's swing, it has zero __potential__ energy, and the maximum amount of __kinetic__ energy. As the pendulum bob swings upward, the potential energy __increases__ and the kinetic energy __decreases__. The pendulum eventually stops swinging because of __friction__ between the pendulum and the __air__. The pendulum's energy is changed into another form, __thermal energy__, and the pendulum bob would be __warmer__ to the touch. According to Albert Einstein, __mass__ is another form of potential energy, called its __rest__ energy. If an object is distorted, the energy that is used to distort the object increases the object's __mass__ slightly.

Analyzing Collisions

When two objects collide, their __shapes__ change slightly. In this change, kinetic energy is changed into __potential__ energy. After the collision, the energy is changed back into __kinetic__ energy. If __all__ of the kinetic energy that was present before the collision is changed into kinetic energy again, the collision is said to be elastic. In this collision, momentum is __conserved__. If __some__ of the kinetic energy that was present before the collision is changed into kinetic energy again, the collision is said to be inelastic. Some of the energy is changed into __other forms__. In an inelastic collision, momentum is __conserved__.

DATE ________ PERIOD ________ NAME ________________________________

CHAPTER 12 Study Guide

Fill in the blanks as you study the chapter.

12.1 TEMPERATURE AND THERMAL ENERGY

What Makes a Hot Body Hot?

Matter is made up of tiny _particles_ that are constantly _moving_. The particles in an object that is _hot_ move faster than the particles in an object that is _cold_. The idea that particles in an object are in motion is the _kinetic molecular_ theory. The particles in a solid are held together by _electromagnetic_ forces. Because the particles are vibrating, they have _kinetic_ energy. However, the particles also have _potential_ energy. The _sum_ of these two amounts of energy makes up the internal, or _thermal_, energy of the object.

Thermal Energy and Temperature

An object that is _hot_ has more thermal energy than a similar object that is _cold_. The particles in a hot object have _more_ kinetic and potential _energy_ than the particles in a cold object. Because particles show a range of energies, it is the _average_ energy of particles that is higher in a(n) _hot_ object than in a(n) _cold_ one. The temperature of a(n) _gas_ is proportional to the average _kinetic_ energy of the particles. The temperature of a(n) _solid_ or a(n) _liquid_ is approximately proportional to the average _kinetic_ energy of the particles. Temperature does not depend on the _number_ of particles in the object. Thermal energy does depend on the _number_ of particles in the object.

Equilibrium and Thermometry

When a glass thermometer is placed into a hot liquid, the particles in the _liquid_ hit the particles in the _glass_, transferring _energy_. As the particles in the glass of the thermometer gain energy, they begin to transfer energy to the _liquid_, and the liquid and thermometer are in thermal _equilibrium_. At this time, the thermometer and the liquid are at the same _temperature_, although they may have different amounts of _thermal energy_. A thermometer depends on a _property_ that changes with temperature. In an alcohol thermometer, the _volume_ of the alcohol increases with temperature. In a liquid crystal thermometer, the _color_ of the crystals changes with temperature. Each kind of crystal in the thermometer changes _color_ at a different _temperature_.

CHAPTER 12 Study Guide NAME ________________________________

Temperature Scales: Celsius and Kelvin

Anders Celsius based a temperature scale on the properties of _water_. On the Celsius scale, the _freezing_ point of water is 0°C, and the _boiling_ point of water is 100°C. Temperatures do not seem to have a(n) _upper_ limit, but they do have a(n) _lower_ limit. This limit is called _absolute zero_, and is the basis of the _Kelvin_ scale. On this scale, the symbol K stands for the _Kelvin_, which is equal to one _Celsius_ degree. The freezing point of _water_ is 273.15 K. The boiling point of water is _373.15 K_.

Heat and Thermal Energy

When a body is placed in contact with a hotter body, the temperature of the cooler body _increases_, because _energy_ flows from the hotter body to the cooler one. Heat is the _energy_ that flows as a result of a difference in _temperature_. Heat is represented by the symbol _Q_, and is measured in _joules_. _Thermal energy_ is the energy that an object contains, but _heat_ is the energy that is transferred between objects. When heat flows into an object, the object's _thermal energy_ and _temperature_ increase. The amount of increase depends on the _mass_ and specific heat of the object. The specific heat of a material is the amount of _energy_ that must be added to _raise_ the temperature of a unit mass _one_ temperature unit. Specific heat is represented by the symbol _C_, and is measured in _J/kg•K_. Compared to most other materials, the specific heat of water is _high_. The heat gained or lost by an object as its temperature changes can be calculated using the equation _$Q = mC\Delta t$_. In this equation, _Q_ is the amount of heat lost or gained, _m_ is the mass of the object, _C_ is the specific heat of the substance, and _Δt_ is the change in temperature.

Calorimetry: Measuring Specific Heat

A calorimeter is used to measure changes in _thermal energy_. A measured _mass_ of a substance is heated to a known _temperature_, and added to a known mass of _water_ at a known temperature in a calorimeter. The temperature of the _water_ increases. The change in thermal energy is calculated from the temperature change of the _water_. The calorimeter is insulated so that _energy_ will be conserved in a closed, isolated _system_. Because the heated object loses thermal energy, its energy change is _negative_. Because the water gains energy, its energy change is _positive_.

NAME ______________________

12.2 CHANGE OF STATE AND LAWS OF THERMODYNAMICS

Change of State

If the temperature of a solid is raised, it changes to a(n) **liquid** and then to a(n) **gas**. This occurs because a(n) **increase** in thermal energy of a solid increases the **kinetic** and **potential** energies of the particles. As the solid is heated, its particles cannot be held in place by the **forces** among them. When the particles are moving freely enough to slide past each other, the substance has changed from a(n) **solid** to a(n) **liquid**. The **temperature** at which this change occurs is the melting point of the substance. During the melting process, the **potential** energy of the particles increases, but the temperature **does not change**. The amount of energy needed to **melt** one **kilogram** of a substance is called the heat of fusion of the substance. For an object at its melting point, adding this energy changes the object's **state**, but not its **temperature**. If the substance is heated after melting is complete, the temperature **increases**. When the temperature reaches the **boiling point**, another change of state takes place. During this change of state the temperature **stays the same**. The amount of **energy** needed to vaporize one **gram** of a liquid is called the heat of **vaporization**. The amount of heat needed to melt a solid is calculated using the equation $Q = mH_f$. In this equation, Q stands for heat, m stands for the mass of the solid, and H_f stands for the heat of fusion. The amount of heat needed to vaporize a liquid is calculated using the equation $Q = mH_v$. In this equation, H_v stands for **heat of vaporization**. To melt a solid or vaporize a liquid, heat must be **added**. To condense a gas or freeze a liquid, heat must be **removed**.

The First Law of Thermodynamics

The thermal energy of an object can be increased if heat is transferred to it or if work is done on it, changing mechanical energy into thermal energy. Other forms of energy that can be converted into thermal energy include light, sound, and electrical energy. The first law of thermodynamics states that the total increase in the thermal energy of a system is the sum of the work done on it and the heat added to it. The first law of thermodynamics is another way of stating the law of conservation of energy. A device that converts thermal energy to mechanical energy continuously is called a heat engine. Heat engines require a high temperature source from which thermal energy can be removed, and a low temperature sink into which thermal energy can be delivered. In an automobile engine, a mixture of air and gasoline is ignited, producing a high temperature flame. The air in the cylinder is heated and it expands, pushing on a(n) piston. This push changes thermal energy into mechanical energy. Some of the thermal energy does not get converted, but instead heats the exhaust gases and engine parts. This thermal energy is transferred out of the engine and is called waste heat. The heat from the flame is equal to the sum of the mechanical energy produced by the engine and the waste heat expelled from the engine. A refrigerator is a device that

NAME ______________________

removes thermal energy from a cooler body and transfers it to a warmer body. An external source of energy is needed to cause the transfer. A fluid, such as Freon is used to transfer heat from the food in the refrigerator to the air in the room. A heat pump is a refrigerator that can be run in two directions. In summer, heat is transferred from the house to the outside air. In the winter, heat is transferred from the outside air to the house. Both transfers require the use of mechanical energy.

The Second Law of Thermodynamics

Sadi Carnot proved that all engines produce waste heat. This is because all systems contain some disorder, or entropy. When heat energy is added to a system, particles move in a random way. The increase in motion of particles increases the entropy of the system. The second law of thermodynamics states that natural processes go in a direction that increases the total entropy of the universe. When two objects of different temperatures are brought together, they reach thermal equilibrium, and their temperatures are the same. The entropy of the system at its final temperature is greater than the entropy of the system before reaching the final temperature. Entropy is often used as a measure of the unavailability of energy. Because the waste heat from an engine or a furnace cannot be used to do work, the energy is not considered to be available.

DATE ______ PERIOD ______ NAME ____________________

CHAPTER 13 Study Guide

Fill in the blanks as you study the chapter.

13.1 THE FLUID STATE

Pressure

A fluid is any material that __flows__ and offers little resistance to a change in its shape when under __pressure__. Fluids include __gases__ and __liquids__. According to the __kinetic molecular__ theory, gases are made up of __particles__ that are in constant __random__ motion, and make __elastic__ collisions with one another and with their container. The pressure that a gas exerts on its container is the result of __collisions__ between gas particles and the walls of the container. Pressure is the __force__ exerted on a unit __area__. Pressure can be calculated using the equation __$p = F/A$__. In this equation, p stands for __pressure__, A stands for __area__, and F stands for __force__. The SI unit of pressure is the __pascal__, which is represented by the symbol __Pa__. A force of one __newton__ acting over one __square meter__ produces a pressure of one pascal. One __kilopascal__ is equal to 1000 Pa.

Fluids at Rest—Hydrostatics

In an ideal fluid, there is no __friction__ among the particles of the fluid. Blaise Pascal noted that the __shape__ of a container does not affect the pressure at any given __depth__. According to Pascal's principle, any change in __pressure__ applied to a fluid in a container is __transmitted__ throughout the fluid. Pascal's principle is the basis for __hydraulic__ systems, in which a fluid is used to __multiply__ a force. The fluid in a hydraulic system is in two chambers, each of which contains a movable __piston__. The force that is transmitted through the system can be calculated by using the equation $F_2 = \frac{F_1A_2}{A_1}$. In this equation, __F_1__ and __F_2__ represent the two forces; __A_1__ and __A_2__ represent the areas of the two pistons. Pressure is proportional to the __depth__ and __density__ of the fluid. For an object immersed in a fluid, there is a net force in a(n) __upward__ direction exerted by the fluid. This force is called the __buoyant__ force. The volume of the immersed object is equal to the __volume__ of the fluid that is displaced. The buoyant force is equal to the __weight__ of the fluid that is displaced. This relationship is known as __Archimedes' principle__. The buoyant force depends only on the weight of the __displaced liquid__, not the weight of the __object__. If the density of an object is greater than the density of the fluid in which it is placed, the object will __sink__. If the density of the object is less than the density of the fluid in which it is placed, the object will __float__.

Fluids in Motion—Hydrodynamics

The relationship between the __velocity__ of a fluid and the __pressure__ exerted by the fluid is described by __Bernoulli's__ principle. Airfoils are devices that use this principle to produce __lift__ when moving through a(n) __fluid__. An airplane wing is curved so that the __top__ surface has a greater curve than the

__bottom__ surface. Air moving over the top of the wing moves a(n) __greater__ distance, and therefore travels at a(n) __greater__ speed. The air pressure over the wing is __less than__ the pressure under the wing. There is a net force in a(n) __upward__ direction. This force is called __lift__. The __flow__ of a fluid can be represented by streamlines. The closer the streamlines are to each other, the greater the __velocity__ and the lower the __pressure__ of the fluid. Streamlines that swirl indicate that the fluid is __turbulent__, and that __Bernoulli's principle__ does not apply to the situation.

Liquids vs Gases

Unlike a gas, a liquid has a(n) __definite__ volume. A gas is __more__ compressible than a liquid. The particles in a liquid are __closer together__ than the particles in a gas. The particles in a liquid exert __electromagnetic__ forces of attraction called __cohesive__ forces.

Surface Tension

The __cohesive__ forces among the particles in a liquid cause the surface of a liquid to have the __smallest__ possible area. This tendency causes the phenomenon known as the __surface tension__ of a liquid. Within a liquid, there is no __net force__ acting on the particles. At the surface there is a net force acting in a(n) __downward__ direction, causing the surface layer of particles to be __compressed__. Liquids form spherical drops because the sphere is the shape that has the __least__ surface for a given volume. Adhesion is an attractive force between particles of __different__ substances. Adhesion causes capillary action, which is the __rising__ of water inside a narrow __tube__.

Evaporation and Condensation

In a liquid, the particles move at __random__ speeds. Only a particle that is near the __surface__ and moving __fast__ can escape from the liquid. This escape is called __evaporation__. As particles escape, the remaining liquid becomes __cooler__, because the average __kinetic energy__ of the remaining particles is decreased. A volatile liquid evaporates __faster__ than a liquid that is not volatile. If a water molecule in the air strikes a cool surface, the molecule may lose __kinetic energy__ and remain on the cool surface. The water is said to have __condensed__ on the surface. Fog forms when water vapor in the air __condenses__ on particles of __dust__ in the air.

Plasma

If the temperature of a gas is increased enough, the __collisions__ between the particles become violent and __electrons__ are pulled off the atoms. The state of matter that is produced is called __plasma__, and contains positively-charged __ions__ and negatively-charged __electrons__. The main difference between a gas and a plasma is that only the __plasma__ can conduct electricity.

CHAPTER 13 Study Guide

NAME ______

13.2 THE SOLID STATE

Solid Bodies

When the temperature of a liquid is lowered, the average kinetic energy of particles _decreases_. The particles move _slower_, and become _frozen_ into a fixed pattern. In a crystal lattice, the only motion of particles is _vibration_ around fixed positions. In an amorphous solid, the particles are in _fixed_ positions, but a(n) _variable_ pattern. An amorphous solid can be classified as a viscous _liquid_. For most substances, the solid state is _more_ dense than the liquid state. However, water is an exception to this rule, reaching its greatest density at a temperature of _4°C_. For most liquids, the freezing point _increases_ as the pressure on the liquid increases. _Water_ is an exception to this rule.

Elasticity of Solids

A(n) _external_ force may cause an object to twist or bend out of shape. Elasticity is the ability of an object to _return_ to its original shape after the external force is _removed_. If the object does not return to its original form, its _elastic limit_ has been reached. Elasticity depends on _electromagnetic_ forces. Malleability is the ability to be rolled into a _sheet_. Ductility is the ability to be drawn into a _wire_.

Thermal Expansion of Matter

Most materials _expand_ when heated and _contract_ when cooled, a property known as _thermal expansion_. This property causes _convection_ currents in fluids. When a solid is heated, its particles vibrate _more_ violently, which _decreases_ the forces of attraction between particles and _increases_ the separation between particles. The change in length of a solid is proportional to its change in _temperature_ and to its _length_. The change in _length_ can be calculated using the equation $\Delta L = \alpha L_1 \Delta T$. In this equation, _$\Delta L$_ stands for the change in length, _L_1_ stands for the initial length, and _ΔT_ stands for the change in temperature. The symbol α stands for the _coefficient of linear expansion_. The _bimetallic_ strips used in thermostat switches make use of thermal expansion. The side of the strip that expands more is on the _outside_ of the curve when the strip is heated, and on the _inside_ of the curve when the strip is cooled.

DATE ______ PERIOD ______ NAME ______

CHAPTER 14 Study Guide

Fill in the blanks as you study the chapter.

14.1 WAVE PROPERTIES

Types of Waves

Water waves and sound waves are _mechanical_ waves. These waves require a(n) _material_ medium. Light waves and radio waves are _electromagnetic_ waves. These waves require _no_ medium. Electrons and other _particles_ show wave-like properties, called _matter_ waves. There are _three_ kinds of mechanical waves. In a transverse wave, particles of the medium vibrate _perpendicular_ to the direction of the _motion_ of the wave. In a longitudinal wave, particles of the medium vibrate _parallel_ to the direction of the _motion_ of the wave. _Surface_ waves are a mixture of transverse and longitudinal waves. In these waves, particles of the medium vibrate _parallel_ and _perpendicular_ to the direction of the wave. A wave pulse is a(n) _single_ disturbance that travels through a medium. A traveling wave is a(n) _continuous_ wave produced by a source that is _vibrating_ with simple _harmonic_ motion.

The Measures of a Wave: Frequency, Wavelength, and Velocity

The period of a wave is the _shortest_ time interval in which the _motion_ repeats itself. The frequency of a wave is the number of complete _vibrations_ per _second_ measured at a fixed location. Frequency is measured in units called _hertz_, which are represented by _Hz_. One vibration per second is equal to one _hertz_. The frequency and period of a wave are related in the equation _$f = 1/T$_. In this equation, _T_ stands for time and _f_ stands for frequency. The shortest distance between points where the wave pattern repeats itself is the _wavelength_ of the wave, and is represented by the Greek letter _λ_. The _high_ points of each wave are called crests, and the _low_ points are called troughs. The velocity of a wave can be calculated by using the equation _$v = \lambda f$_.

Amplitude of a Wave

The _maximum_ displacement from the rest, or _equilibrium_, position is the amplitude of a wave. It takes _more_ work to produce a wave with a large amplitude than it does to produce a wave with a small amplitude. The larger the amplitude of the wave, the more _energy_ is transferred.

NAME ____________

14.2 WAVE INTERFERENCE

Waves at Boundaries Between Media

The speed of a mechanical wave does not depend on the _amplitude_ or the _frequency_ of the wave. It only depends on the _properties_ of the medium. In a given medium, the speed of a wave with a large amplitude is _equal to_ the speed of a wave with a small amplitude. In a given medium, the speed of a high-frequency wave is _equal to_ the speed of a low-frequency wave. When a wave reaches a boundary between one medium and another, the wave that reaches the boundary is called the _incident_ wave. The wave that moves through the new medium is called the _transmitted_ wave. Some of the _energy_ of the incident wave moves backward from the boundary and is called the _reflected_ wave. If the difference between the two media is small, _most_ of the energy of the incident wave will be transmitted. If the difference between the two media is great, _little_ of the energy will be transmitted. When a wave passes from a less dense to a more dense medium, the reflected wave is _inverted_. When a wave passes from a more dense to a less dense medium, the reflected wave is _erect_. When a wave is transmitted from one medium to another, the _frequency_ of the wave does not change. The _speed_ and the _wavelength_ of the wave do change.

Superposition of Waves

When two or more waves move through a medium, each wave affects the medium _independently_. According to the principle of superposition, the _displacement_ of a medium caused by two or more waves is the algebraic _sum_ of the _displacements_ caused by the individual waves. Interference is the result of the _superposition_ of two or more waves. Constructive interference occurs when the wave displacements are in _the same_ direction, and results in a wave with a(n) _greater_ displacement. After the two pulses have passed each other, they have their original _shape_ and _size_. Destructive interference occurs when the wave displacements are in _opposite_ directions. If the amplitudes of the two pulses are equal but opposite, the displacement produced when the pulses meet is _zero_. If the amplitudes are unequal, _destructive interference_ will not be complete.

Standing Waves

When two waves meet, a point in the medium that is always _undisturbed_ by the wave is called a node. A node is produced by _destructive_ interference. When two waves meet, the point in the medium where there is the greatest _displacement_ is called an antinode. An antinode is produced by _constructive_ interference. If the period of a wave is equal to the time it takes for the wave to travel to a fixed point and back, a(n) _standing_ wave is produced. In this wave, the nodes and antinodes are _stationary_ and the wave appears to be _standing still_.

NAME ____________

Reflection of Waves

The direction of waves moving in two or three dimensions is shown by _ray_ diagrams. The ray that reaches a barrier is called the _incident_ ray. The ray that moves back from the barrier is called the _reflected_ ray. The direction of the barrier is shown by a line drawn at a(n) _right angle_ to the barrier. This line is called the _normal_. The angle between the _incident_ ray and the _normal_ is called the angle of incidence. The angle between the _reflected_ ray and the _normal_ is called the angle of reflection. The law of _reflection_ states that the angle of incidence equals the angle of reflection.

Refraction of Waves

In water waves, the velocity is _slower_ in shallower water. If the incident ray is parallel to the normal, there is a change in the velocity and _wavelength_ of the wave. If the incident ray is not parallel to the normal, there is a change in velocity, wavelength, and _direction_ of the wave. The change in _direction_ of a wave at the boundary between two media is called refraction.

Diffraction and Interference of Waves

When waves reach a small opening in a barrier, they form _circular_ waves that spread out from the opening. This spreading of waves is called _diffraction_. The smaller the _wavelength_ in comparison to the size of the barrier, the _less_ the diffraction. When there are two openings in a barrier, _two_ sets of circular waves are produced. When the new waves interfere with each other, _constructive_ interference produces large waves, and _destructive_ interference produces a line of nodes.

DATE ______ PERIOD ______ NAME ____________

CHAPTER 15 Study Guide

Fill in the blanks as you study the chapter.

15.1 PROPERTIES OF SOUND

Sound Waves

Sound waves are __longitudinal__ waves, produced by the __compression__ and __rarefaction__ of matter. In air, sound waves are produced when a vibrating __source__ causes regular variations in __air pressure__. The __frequency__ of a sound wave is the number of oscillations in __air pressure__ each second. The __velocity__ of sound in air depends on air temperature. In solids and liquids, the velocity of air is __greater than__ it is in gases. Sounds cannot travel through a(n) __vacuum__. Sound waves can be __reflected__ by a hard surface, causing a(n) __echo__. The reflection of sound waves can be used to find the __distance__ between a source and a reflector. Ships that are equipped with __sonar__ make use of sound reflection. Sound waves can be __diffracted__ when they pass through a narrow opening. Sound waves can __interfere__ and produce nodes where little sound is heard. The __wavelength__ is the distance between adjacent regions of maximum __pressure__. The equation that relates velocity, frequency, and wavelength is __$v = \lambda f$__.

The Doppler Shift

The Doppler shift causes sounds to seem __higher__ in frequency when the source is moving toward the listener, and __lower__ in frequency when the source is moving away from the listener. The __frequency__ of the source of the sound does not change. The Doppler shift is used in the __radar__ that measures the speed of automobiles. It is also used in astronomy to measure the __speed__ of galaxies and infer the __distance__ to them.

Pitch and Loudness

The __frequency__ of a sound wave is heard as pitch. The __amplitude__ of a sound wave is heard as loudness. The notes of the musical scale have different __frequencies__. Notes with frequencies that give ratios of small __whole__ numbers sound pleasing when heard together. Notes in a ratio of 2:1 are said to be a(n) __octave__ apart. Sound levels are measured in __decibels__ and indicate sound __pressure__. Sound level is a ratio of the __sound pressure__ of a given sound wave to the __sound pressure__ of the most __faintly__ heard sound level.

CHAPTER 15 Study Guide NAME ____________

15.2 THE SOUND OF MUSIC

Sources of Sound

Sound is produced by a(n) __vibrating__ object. The human voice is produced when the __vocal cords__ vibrate. The frequency of the vibration is controlled by the __muscles__ that put tension on the vocal cords. In a trumpet, the __player's lips__ vibrate. In a clarinet, the __reed__ vibrates. In a flute, a column of __air__ vibrates. In a guitar, the __strings__ vibrate.

Resonance

In a trumpet or clarinet, sound is heard only when the __air__ in the tube of the instrument vibrates at the same __frequency__ as the lips or reed. This effect is called __resonance__. The pitch of the instrument is changed by changing the __length__ of the column of vibrating __air__. A closed pipe is a resonating tube with __one end__ closed. When sound waves reflected through the pipe reinforce each other, a(n) __standing__ wave is produced. There is a pressure __antinode__ at the point of reflection, and a pressure __node__ at the open end of the tube. The shortest closed pipe that can produce a standing wave is __one-fourth wavelength__ long. An open pipe resonator has both ends __open__. There is a pressure __node__ at each end, and at least one pressure __antinode__ between. The shortest open pipe that can produce a standing wave is __one-half wavelength__ long.

Detection of Sound

Sound detectors convert the __kinetic__ energy of air molecules into __another form of__ energy. The __ear__ is the sound detector of the human body. It consists of three parts: the __outer ear__, __middle ear__, and __inner ear__. The __outer__ ear collects sound. The sound causes the __eardrum__ to vibrate. Then three __bones__ in the __middle__ ear vibrate. The vibrations are transmitted to the oval window in the __inner__ ear. In the __cochlea__, fluid vibrates, which causes tiny hair cells to vibrate and stimulate __nerve cells__. The sensation is interpreted by the __brain__. Older people are __less__ sensitive to high frequencies than are young people. Exposure to __loud sounds__ can cause the ear to lose sensitivity to sounds because of damage to the __hair cells__ in the inner ear.

The Quality of Sound

Most sounds are made up of several __frequencies__. The quality of the sound depends on the relative __intensities__ of the frequencies. Sound quality is called __timbre__. If two waves of slightly different frequencies reach the ear, the __sum__ of the two waves has a(n) __amplitude__ that oscillates in intensity. The listener hears a pulsing variation in __loudness__, called a(n) __beat__. The frequency of the __beats__ is the __difference__ in the frequencies of the two waves. If there are more beats than the ear can distinguish, the ear detects a __complex__ wave. If the sound is __unpleasant__, it is called a dissonance. If the sound is __pleasant__, it is called a consonance, or a(n) __chord__. Musical instruments

CHAPTER 15 Study Guide

NAME

that have pipe resonators produce sounds that have more than one resonant frequency. The lowest of these frequencies is called the fundamental, and whole-number multiples of the lowest frequency are called harmonics. An open-pipe resonator produces the fundamental and all harmonics. A closed-pipe resonator produces the fundamental and odd harmonics. Sound distortion occurs when sounds of different frequencies are transmitted with different efficiencies. Noise consists of many different frequencies with no relationship. If all frequencies have equal amplitudes, the result is called white noise. The resonator of the human voice is the throat and mouth cavity. The shape of the resonator is changed by the movements of the tongue and teeth, and changes the number of harmonics present.

DATE ______ PERIOD ______ NAME ______

CHAPTER 16 Study Guide

Fill in the blanks as you study the chapter.

16.1 LIGHT FUNDAMENTALS

The Facts of Light

Light is the range of frequencies of electromagnetic waves that stimulates the retina of the eye. The shortest wavelengths of light are about 400 nm long and are violet in color. The longest wavelengths of light are about 700 nm long, and are red in color. In a vacuum or uniform medium, light travels in a(n) straight line. This description of the path of light is the ray model. A ray is a straight line that represents the path of a very narrow beam of light. Ray optics is the use of ray diagrams to study light and describe how it is reflected and refracted.

The Speed of Light

Galileo was the first person to hypothesize that light has a finite speed, although he was unable to measure it. The first measurement of the speed of light was made by Roemer, who made measurements based on one of the moons of Jupiter. The speed of light is the product of its frequency and wavelength. The equation that shows this relationship is $c = f$. The symbol used to represent the speed of light is c. The International Committee on Weights and Measures has defined the speed of light in a vacuum to be exactly 299 792 458 m/s. Expressed to three significant figures, the speed of light is 3.00×10^8 m/s.

Sources of Light

A body that emits light waves is said to be luminous and a body that reflects light waves is said to be illuminated. An incandescent object is a(n) luminous body that gives off light as a result of being hot. The rate at which light is emitted by a source is luminous flux, which is represented by P, and is expressed in a unit called the lumen. The illumination of a surface is called the illuminance, which is measured in lumens per square meter, or lux. If the distance from a surface to a point source of light is doubled, the illumination reaching the surface is one-fourth as great. The candela is a measure of luminous intensity. Luminous intensity is equal to luminous flux divided by 4π. To increase the illumination on a surface, increase the luminous flux of the light source or decrease the distance between the source and the surface. The equation used to determine illuminance is $E = \frac{P}{4\pi d^2}$. In this equation, E represents illuminance, P represents the luminous flux of the source, and d represents the distance from the surface. This equation is only valid if a line that points to the bulb is perpendicular to the source and if the source can be considered to be a point source.

CHAPTER 16 Study Guide

NAME ______

16.2 LIGHT AND MATTER

Color

Materials that transmit light waves are described as transparent. Materials that transmit light waves, but do not permit objects to be seen clearly, are described as translucent. Materials that are described as opaque absorb or reflect the light waves that fall on them. The arrangement of colors from violet to red is called the spectrum, and was named by Newton, who showed that white light is made up of colors. Each color is associated with a specific wavelength. In the additive color process, adding together red, green, and blue light produces white light. These three colors are called the primary colors of light. When two of the primary colors are mixed, a secondary color of light is formed. These three colors are yellow, cyan, and magenta. For each primary color there is a(n) secondary color that is its complementary color. Complementary colors add to form white light. The complementary color of red is cyan. Dyes and pigments absorb certain wavelengths and transmit or reflect other wavelengths. If all wavelengths are absorbed, no light is reflected and an object appears black. The absorption of light forms colors by the subtractive process. A(n) primary pigment absorbs one color. A(n) secondary pigment absorbs two colors. Yellow and cyan are two of the primary pigments. Red and blue are two of the secondary pigments. When complementary pigments are combined, the result is black.

Formation of Colors in Thin Films

The colors seen in a soap bubble are caused by constructive and destructive interference of light waves. This occurs because the thickness of a soap film varies. Some light is reflected by the surface of the film and some light is transmitted. The transmitted light is reflected by the back surface of the film. The reflected waves of some wavelengths reinforce each other, while the waves of other wavelengths interfere with each other. As a result, each color of light is reinforced by a different area of the film.

Polarization of Light

Only transverse waves can be polarized. The waves in a beam of light vibrate in every direction perpendicular to the direction of travel. A polarizing filter allows the waves vibrating in one plane to pass through, and the light is said to be polarized. If the plane of a second polarizing filter is perpendicular to the plane of the first, no light passes through the second filter. If the plane of the second filter is parallel to the plane of the first, most of the light will be transmitted.

DATE ______ PERIOD ______ NAME ______

CHAPTER 17 Study Guide

Fill in the blanks as you study the chapter.

17.1 HOW LIGHT BEHAVES AT A BOUNDARY

The Law of Reflection

When a light ray strikes a reflecting surface, the angle of reflection is equal to the angle of incidence. Both angles are measured from a(n) normal, which is perpendicular to the reflecting surface. When a beam of light strikes a rough surface, it reflects in many directions, producing a(n) diffuse reflection. When a beam of light strikes a smooth surface, the reflected rays are parallel to each other, producing a(n) regular reflection.

Refraction of Light

The bending of light at the boundary between two media is called refraction. The angle of incidence is measured between the incident ray and the normal. The angle of refraction is measured between the refracted ray and the normal. Refraction does not occur if the angle of incidence is zero. When this happens, the ray changes speed but it does not change direction. As a light ray enters a more optically dense medium, its speed decreases, and the refracted ray bends toward the normal. As a light ray passes into a medium in which it travels faster, the refracted ray bends away from the normal.

Snell's Law

Snell's law states that a ray of light bends in such a way that the ratio of the sine of the angle of incidence to the sine of the angle of refraction is a constant. This constant is called the index of refraction if the light is moving from a(n) vacuum to another medium. For a ray traveling from one medium into another, Snell's law is written as the equation, $n_i \sin\theta_i = n_r \sin\theta_r$. In the equation, n_i is the index of refraction of the incident medium and n_r is the index of refraction of the second medium. The angle of incidence is represented by θ_i and the angle of refraction is represented by θ_r.

Index of Refraction and the Speed of Light

The speed of light depends on the medium in which it travels. The index of refraction is a measure of the amount that light bends when passing into the medium from a(n) vacuum. The index of refraction can be calculated by comparing the speed of light in a vacuum to the speed of light in the medium. The equation for this is $n_s = c/v_s$.

CHAPTER 17 Study Guide

NAME ______

17.2 APPLICATIONS OF REFLECTED AND REFRACTED LIGHT

Total Internal Reflection

Total internal reflection occurs when light passes from a(n) __more__ optically dense medium to a(n) __less__ optically dense medium at an angle so great that there is no __refracted__ ray. The critical angle is the __incident__ angle that causes the refracted ray to lie along the __boundary__ of the substance. If the angle of incidence is greater than the critical angle, the incident ray cannot be __refracted__, but instead is __reflected__. Light is internally reflected in optical fibers because the main glass fiber is coated with a glass that has a(n) __lower__ index of refraction.

Effects of Refraction

A mirage of a puddle is seen on a road if the road is very __hot__. The road heats the air above it, which changes the __index of refraction__ of the air. A ray of light aimed toward the road is bent __away from__ the normal, and more __parallel__ to the road. An object submerged in a liquid may appear to be __closer to__ the surface of the liquid than it really is. Light is refracted by the atmosphere so that sunlight is visible __before__ sunrise and __after__ sunset.

Dispersion of Light

The index of refraction depends on the __wavelength__ of the incident light. In most materials, red light travels __fastest__ and has the __smallest__ index of refraction. Violet light travels __slowest__ and has the __largest__ index of refraction. As a result, red light is bent __less than__ violet light. This difference causes light leaving a prism to be dispersed into a(n) __spectrum__. Different light sources have different __spectra__, which can be studied by dispersing the light with a prism. Water droplets in the air act as prisms, refracting each color at a(n) __different__ angle. In each water droplet, light is __refracted__ as it enters, __reflected__ inside the droplet, and __refracted__ again as it leaves the droplet.

DATE ______ PERIOD ______ NAME ______

CHAPTER 18 Study Guide

Fill in the blanks as you study the chapter.

18.1 MIRRORS

Objects and Their Images in Plane Mirrors

A plane mirror is a(n) __flat__, smooth surface that reflects light in a(n) __regular__ way. When light rays are reflected from a plane mirror, they __spread out__. The light rays can be extended __behind__ the mirror. The image is located where the extended light rays __apparently intersect__. The image is virtual because there is __no__ light at that point. The distance from the object to the mirror is __equal to__ the distance from the image to the mirror. The size of the image is __equal to__ the size of the object. The position of the image is __erect__, and the __left__ and __right__ appear to be reversed. Actually, the __front__ and __back__ are reversed.

Concave Mirrors

A concave mirror reflects light from its __inner__ surface. In a spherical concave mirror, the center of the sphere is called the __center of curvature__. The line from this point to the center of the surface of the mirror is the __principal axis__ of the mirror. Parallel light rays __converge__ at the focal point, which is __half__ the distance between the mirror and the center of curvature. The focal length of a concave mirror is the distance from the __focal point__ to the surface of the mirror, along the __principal axis__. The focal length is __half__ the radius of curvature of the mirror.

Spherical Aberration and Parabolic Mirrors

Parallel light rays converge at the focal point if they are close to the __principal axis__ of the mirror. Other parallel light rays converge slightly __closer to__ the mirror. This difference causes the effect known as __spherical aberration__. To avoid this effect, use a curved mirror that is __parabolic__ in shape. These mirrors can also produce a beam of parallel light rays if the source of the light is placed at the __focal point__ of the mirror.

Real vs Virtual Images

An image is real if light rays __converge__ and then __pass through__ the image. A real image __can__ be projected on a screen. An image is virtual if light rays do not __converge__, but appear to __diverge__ from a point behind the mirror. A virtual image __cannot__ be projected on a screen.

Real Images Formed by Concave Mirrors

The real image of an object beyond the center of curvature of a concave mirror is located between the _center of curvature_ and the _focal point_ of the mirror. The size of the image is _smaller than_ the size of the object, and the position of the image is _inverted_. As the object is moved inward toward the center of curvature, the image moves _outward_ toward the _center of curvature_. If the object is at the center of curvature the real image is at the _center of curvature_. The size of the image is _equal to_ the size of the object, and the position of the image is _inverted_. The mirror equation, $\frac{1}{f} = \frac{1}{d_i} + \frac{1}{d_o}$, can be used to predict the location of an image. In this equation, f represents the _focal length_, d_i represents the distance from the _image_ to the mirror, and d_o represents the distance from the _object_ to the mirror. The ratio of the size of the _image_ to the size of the _object_ is the magnification of the mirror. The magnification equation is $m = \frac{h_i}{h_o} = \frac{-d_i}{d_o}$. In this equation, _$m$_ represents magnification, d_i and d_o are the same as in the mirror equation, h_i represents the _size of the image_, and h_o represents the _size of the object_. If d_i and d_o are both positive, then both _m_ and _h_i_ are negative, which means the position of the image is _inverted_.

Virtual Images Formed by Concave Mirrors

If the object is at the focal point, the reflected rays are _parallel_, and the image is said to be at _infinity_. If the object is between the focal point and the mirror, the _virtual_ image is located _behind_ the mirror. The size of the image is _greater than_ the size of the object, and the position of the image is _erect_.

Virtual Images Formed by Convex Mirrors

A convex mirror reflects light from its _outer_ surface. Rays reflected from this surface always _diverge_, so they do not form _real_ images. The focal point of a convex mirror is located _behind_ the mirror. In calculations, the focal length of a convex mirror is a(n) _negative_ number. A convex mirror always produces a(n) _virtual_ image. The size of the image is _less than_ the size of the object, and the position of the image is _erect_.

18.2 LENSES

Types of Lenses

A lense is made of a(n) _transparent_ material. The refractive index of the lens material is _greater than_ the refractive index of air. At least one surface of a lens is part of a(n) _sphere_. The other surface may be _curved_ or it may be _flat_. A convex lens is _thicker_ at the center than at the edges. A convex lens is called a(n) _converging_ lens because it refracts parallel rays so that they _meet_. A concave lens is _thinner_ at the center than at the edges. This lens is called a(n) _diverging_ lens because it refracts light rays so that they _spread out_.

Real Images Formed by Convex Lenses

The principal axis of a lens is a line _perpendicular_ to the plane of the lens that passes through its _midpoint_. Parallel rays converge at the _focal point_ of the lens. The focal length of the lens depends on its _shape_ and on the _refractive index_ of the material used to make the lens. Although light is refracted at the two _surfaces_ of the lens, lens drawings often show all refraction occurring at the _principal plane_, which passes through the middle of the lens. If the object is far from the convex lens, a(n) _real_ image is formed. The size of the image is _less than_ the size of the object, and the position of the image is _inverted_. If the object is close to, but outside, the focal point of the lens, a(n) _real_ image is formed. The size of the image is _greater than_ the size of the object, and the position of the image is _inverted_. If the object is placed twice the focal length from the lens, the image is at _twice_ the focal length from the lens. The size of the image is _equal to_ the size of the object and the position of the object is _inverted_. The lens equation is $\frac{1}{f} = \frac{1}{d_i} + \frac{1}{d_o}$. The magnification equation is $m = \frac{h_i}{h_o} = \frac{-d_i}{d_o}$.

Virtual Images Formed by Convex Lenses

If the object is placed between the focal point and the lens, the light rays do not _converge_ on the other side of the lens. The _virtual_ image appears on the _same_ side of the lens as the object. The size of the image is _greater than_ the size of the object, and the position of the image is _erect_. A convex lens used to produce an enlarged, upright image is called a(n) _magnifying_ glass.

Virtual Images Formed by Concave Lenses

A concave lens always causes light rays to _diverge_. A concave lens always produces a(n) _virtual_ image. The size of the image is _less than_ the size of the object, and the position of the image is _erect_. The focal length of a concave lens is always a(n) _negative_ number.

CHAPTER 18 Study Guide

NAME ______

Chromatic Aberration

The edges of a lens act like a(n) _prism_, and bend different _wavelengths_ of light at different angles. As a result, light that passes through the edge of the lens is slightly _dispersed_, causing a ring of _color_ to be seen through the lens. This effect, called chromatic aberration, always occurs when a(n) _single_ lens is used. It is reduced by combining a convex lens with a(n) _concave_ lens that has a(n) _different_ index of refraction. A lens made in this way is called a(n) _achromatic_ lens.

Optical Instruments

The eye focuses light on the _retina_. Most of the refraction in the eye occurs as light enters the _cornea_. The lens of the eye is made of a(n) _flexible_ material that has a different index of refraction than the _fluid_ inside the eye. Tiny muscles in the eye change the _shape_, and therefore, the focal length of the lens. When the muscles relax, the focal length is _longer_, and _distant_ objects can be focused on the retina. When the muscles contract, the focal length becomes _shorter_, and _near_ objects can be focused on the retina. If a person is nearsighted, or _myopic_, images of distant objects form _in front of_ the retina. Nearsightedness is corrected with _concave_ lenses. If a person is farsighted, images form _behind_ the retina. Farsightedness is corrected with _convex_ lenses. If the eye or the lens is not _spherical_, the person has astigmatism. Contact lenses are placed on the _cornea_ and change the focal length of the eye. Microscopes use at least two _convex_ lenses to focus on small objects. The objective lens has a(n) _short_ focal length, and produces a(n) _real_ image. The eyepiece lens produces a magnified _virtual_ image of the image formed by the objective lens. A telescope is used to focus on _distant_ objects. The objective lens has a(n) _long_ focal length, and the eyepiece lens has a(n) _short_ focal length. The viewer sees a(n) _virtual_ image.

DATE ______ PERIOD ______ NAME ______

CHAPTER 19 Study Guide

Fill in the blanks as you study the chapter.

19.1 WHEN LIGHT WAVES INTERFERE

The Two-Slit Interference Pattern

The edges of shadows are not perfectly _sharp_ because of diffraction, the _bending_ of light waves around the edges of _barriers_. In Thomas Young's experiment, light passed through two _slits_ and was diffracted. The overlapping light produced a pattern of _bright_ and _dark_ bands. These bands are called interference _fringes_. Monochromatic light is light of only one _wavelength_. Monochromatic light that passes through a slit is described as coherent because the waves are all _in step_. When monochromatic light passes through two slits, _constructive_ interference occurs where crests overlap, producing a(n) _bright_ band in the pattern. Where a crest and a trough meet, _destructive_ interference occurs, producing a(n) _dark_ band in the pattern. In this pattern the central band is a(n) _bright_ band. If white light is used instead of monochromatic light, _spectra_ are seen instead of dark and light bands, and the central band is _white_.

Measuring the Wavelength of a Wave

Using double-slit diffraction, _Young_ measured the wavelength of light. The first bright band on either side of the central band is called the _first-order_ line. It is caused by the _constructive_ interference of two waves the paths of which differ by exactly _one wavelength_. The equation used to calculate the wavelength of a light wave is $\lambda = \frac{xd}{L}$. In this equation, _λ_ represents wavelength, _L_ represents the distance between the screen and the slits, _d_ represents the distance between the slits, and _x_ represents the distance between the central band and the first-order line.

Single-Slit Diffraction

The diffraction of light is less noticeable than the diffraction of sound because the wavelengths of light are _smaller_ than the wavelengths of sound. When light passes through a single slit, the pattern seen has a wide _bright_ band in the center with _dimmer_ bright bands on either side. At the central band, all waves are in step, so _constructive_ interference occurs. To the side of the central band, waves _are not_ in step, and so _destructive_ interference occurs, producing a dark band. The next bright band is seen when two waves on paths that differ by one _wavelength_ meet and _constructive_ interference occurs. The equation used to calculate the wavelength of light is $x = \frac{\lambda L}{w}$. In this equation, _λ_ represents wavelength, _L_ represents the distance from the slit to the screen, _w_ represents the width of the slit, _x_ represents the distance from the bright band to the dark band. For a constant slit width, the shorter the wavelength, the _narrower_ the pattern.

CHAPTER 19 Study Guide

NAME ____________

19.2 APPLICATIONS OF DIFFRACTION

Diffraction Gratings

A diffraction grating is a device that has a series of many _slits_. On a glass diffraction grating, the _clear spaces_ between scratched lines serve as the slits. Compared to double-slit diffraction patterns, the patterns produced by a grating have narrower _bright_ bands and wider _dark_ bands. This pattern makes it easier to distinguish individual _colors_. The equation used to calculate wavelength with a diffraction grating is similar to the _double_-slit equation, but the _angle_ between the central band and first-order line is measured instead of the distance between them. The device used for this measurement is called a grating _spectrometer_, and is calibrated so that the _angle_ can be read directly.

Resolving Power of Lenses

Light passing through the lens of a telescope is _diffracted_ by the lens. As a result, the light coming from a star will _spread out_. If two stars are close together, the light from the stars will _overlap_ and will be seen as one star. According to the Rayleigh criterion for _resolution_, the two images are resolved if the central bright band of one star falls on the _first dark_ band of the second star. The effects of diffraction can be reduced in a telescope by using a(n) _larger_ lens. The effects of diffraction in a microscope can be reduced by using a light with a(n) _smaller_ wavelength.

DATE ________ PERIOD ________ NAME ____________

CHAPTER 20 Study Guide

Fill in the blanks as you study the chapter.

20.1 ELECTRICAL CHARGES

Charged Objects

Electrostatics is the study of electrical _charges_ that can be _collected_ and held in one place. The force exerted by charged objects is known to be strong because the _acceleration_ caused by this force is greater than the acceleration caused by _gravitational_ force. The electrical effect and the effect of gravity are different because only the effect of _gravity_ is constant. Two identical objects that have been charged the same way _repel_ each other. Objects that are charged differently _attract_ each other. There are two states of charge, called _positive_ and _negative_. These charges are produced only in _pairs_. Rubbing two objects together _separates_ the charges.

A Microscopic View of Charging

An atom contains light, negatively-charged particles called _electrons_, which surround a positively charged _nucleus_. The positive charge of the nucleus is exactly _balanced_ by the negative charge of the electrons, so the atom is not _charged_. The addition of _energy_ can remove electrons from atoms, leaving behind a(n) _positive_ ion. If the electrons that were removed become attached to another atom, a(n) _negative_ ion is produced. If two objects are rubbed together, electrons from one object are _transferred_ to the second. As a result, the first object has a(n) _positive_ charge and the second object has a(n) _negative_ charge. The total charge on the two objects is _equal to_ the total charge before they were rubbed together, because charges cannot be _created_ or _destroyed_. They can only be _separated_.

Conductors and Insulators

Materials through which charges will not move easily are called electrical _insulators_. Materials that allow charges to move about easily are called electrical _conductors_. Glass is an example of a(n) _insulator_. Metal is an example of a good _conductor_ because at least one _electron_ in each metal atom is free to move throughout the entire piece of metal. Although air is a(n) _insulator_, it conducts a charge if the _forces_ exerted by the charges remove _electrons_ from molecules in the air, forming a conductor called _plasma_.

CHAPTER 20 Study Guide

NAME ______________________

20.2 ELECTRICAL FORCES

Forces on Charged Bodies

The two kinds of electrical charges are __positive__ and __negative__. Charges exert __force__ on __other__ __charges__ over a distance. __Like__ charges repel and __unlike__ charges attract. A device called a(n) __electroscope__ is used to detect charges. When a negatively-charged rod touches the knob of the electroscope, __electrons__ are added to the knob, and spread over all the __metal__ surfaces. The two leaves inside the electroscope become __negatively__ charged, and __repel__ each other. Charging a neutral body by __touching it__ with a charged body is called charging by conduction. If the electroscope is given a positive charge, the leaves become __positively__ charged, and __repel__ each other. To identify the charge on an electroscope, bring an object with known charge __near__ the electroscope. If the leaves move farther apart, the charge on the electroscope is __the same as__ the charge on the object. If the leaves move closer together, the charge on the electroscope is __opposite to__ the charge on the object.

Separation of Charge and Charging by Induction

Electric forces can change insulators into __conductors__. If an uncharged object is brought near a positively charged object, the __negative__ charges in the uncharged object will be __attracted to__ the positively charged object. The uncharged object will still be __neutral__, but the charges will be __separated__. Causing charges to separate without touching the object is called charging by __induction__. The __negative__ charges on the bottom of thunderclouds can separate __charges__ in Earth.

Coulomb's Law

Coulomb's law describes the __force__ between two charged objects. The electric force varies __inversely__ with the __square__ of the distance between the two charged objects. The electric force varies __directly__ with the __product__ of the charges on the objects. Coulomb's law can be written as an equation, $F = \frac{Kqq'}{d^2}$. In this equation, F represents __force__, q and q' represent the __charges__ on the objects, d represents the __distance__ between the objects, and K is a(n) __constant__. The force that one charged object exerts on a second is __equal to__ the magnitude of the force the second object exerts on the first. The two forces are __opposite__ in direction. This relationship between forces is an example of Newton's __third__ law.

CHAPTER 20 Study Guide

NAME ______________________

The Unit of Charge: The Coulomb

Coulomb defined a(n) __standard__ quantity of charge in terms of the amount of __force__ it produces. The SI unit of __charge__ is the Coulomb, abbreviated as __C__. One coulomb is the charge of 6.25×10^{18} __electrons__. The magnitude of the charge of one electron is called the __elementary__ charge. The electric force is a(n) __vector__ quantity, which means it has both __magnitude__ and __direction__. A repulsive force has a(n) __positive__ sign and an attractive force has a(n) __negative__ sign.

Using Electric Forces on Neutral Bodies

A charged object may either __attract__ or __repel__ another charged object. A charged object may only __attract__ an uncharged object. The uncharged object will then __attract__ the charged object. This relationship is an example of Newton's __third__ law. Electric forces are used to collect __neutral__ particles such as soot in smokestacks.

DATE ______ PERIOD ______ NAME ______

CHAPTER 21 Study Guide

Fill in the blanks as you study the chapter.

21.1 CREATING AND MEASURING ELECTRIC FIELDS

The Electric Field

A(n) __charge__ produces an electric field. The electric field can be observed because it produces __forces__ on other __charges__. An electric field is measured by placing a small __positive__ test charge in it. According to __Coulomb's__ law, the force is proportional to the test charge. The equation used to calculate the magnitude of an electric field is $E = \frac{F}{q'}$. In this equation, __*E*__ represents the magnitude of the field, __*F*__ represents the force on the test charge, and __*q'*__ represents the magnitude of the test charge. The magnitude of the field is a(n) __vector__, because it has both magnitude and __direction__. The direction of the electric field is __the same as__ the direction of the force on the positive test charge. The magnitude of the intensity of an electric field is measured in __newtons per coulomb__. To measure the entire field, the __test charge__ is moved to locations throughout the field until all locations have been tested. The total electric field is the vector __sum__ of the fields of the individual charges.

Picturing the Electric Field

When electric field lines are used to show a field, the direction of the field at any point is the __tangent__ drawn to the field line at that point. The __strength__ of the field is indicated by the spacing between the lines, and is __stronger__ where the lines are closer together. Near a positive charge, the direction of the force on a positive test charge is __away from__ the positive charge. Near a negative charge, the direction of the force on a positive test charge is __toward__ the charge. Field lines __do not__ exist, but electric fields __do__ exist. The field provides a way of calculating the __force__ on a charged body. It does not explain why __charged__ bodies exert __forces__ on each other.

CHAPTER 21 Study Guide NAME ______

21.2 APPLICATIONS OF THE ELECTRIC FIELD

Energy and the Electric Potential

Two unlike charges __repel__ each other, so work must be done to move them __farther apart__. When work is done on the charges, it is stored as __potential__ energy. The potential energy of a test charge is called the electric __potential__, and is measured in a unit called the __volt__. The change in potential energy per unit __charge__ is called the electric potential difference. When work is done to move a positive test charge farther from a(n) __negative__ charge, the potential energy of the test charge increases. When the positive test charge is moved back to its original position, its potential energy __decreases__. Only __differences__ in electric potential energy can be measured. Potential differences are measured with a(n) __voltmeter__. When a positive test charge is moved away from a positive charge, the potential energy __decreases__. The electric potential is __greatest__ when the positive test charge is closest to the positive charge.

The Electric Potential in a Uniform Field

The electric field between two __parallel__ plates is uniform. The equation used to calculate the potential difference between two points in a uniform field is __$V = Ed$__. In this equation, __*V*__ represents the potential difference, __*E*__ represents the magnitude of the field, and __*d*__ represents the distance between the points.

Millikan's Oil Drop Experiment

The measurement of the charge of a(n) __electron__ was made by Robert A. Millikan. In this experiment, fine drops of oil were sprayed by a(n) __atomizer__ into the __air__. The drops were charged by __friction__ as they passed through the __atomizer__. The drops fell due to __gravity__. Some of the drops were trapped between two charged parallel __plates__. The potential difference between the plates was adjusted until a charged drop was __suspended__ between the plates. At this point the __downward__ force of the weight of the drop was __equal to__ the __upward__ force of the electric field. Although the drops had a wide variety of charges, the __change__ in the charge were always a multiple of -1.6×10^{-19} C. Millikan concluded that this was the __smallest__ change in charge that could occur, and was equal to the charge of one __electron__.

Sharing of Charge

All systems come to __equilibrium__ when the energy of the system is at a minimum. In an electrical system, this happens when all objects in the system have the same __potential__. In a conductor, charges __move__ until all parts of the conductor have the same potential. If a large sphere and a small sphere have the same charge, the larger sphere will have the __lower__ potential, because charges are __more__ spread out on the larger surface area. If the spheres are touched together, charge will move from the __smaller__

NAME ____

sphere to the _larger_ sphere, until their potentials are equal. When the two spheres are at the same potential, the _larger_ sphere will have the greater charge. Because Earth is such a large sphere, almost any amount of charge can flow into it without changing its _potential_. Thus Earth can absorb _excess_ charges from an object, which is called _grounding_ the object.

Electric Fields Near Conductors

The charges on a conductor spread out as far as possible, which makes the energy of the system as _low_ as possible. If a conductor is solid, all the charges are on the _surface_. If a conductor is hollow, all charges move to the _outer_ surface. A closed metal container _shields_ the inside from electric fields. Charges are _closer together_ at sharp points of a conductor, and the field is _stronger_ at these points. A lightning rod has a(n) _pointed_ shape so that lightning will strike the rod rather than the house. From the rod, the charges flow to the _ground_.

Storing Charges—The Capacitor

As charge is added to an object, the potential between the object and _Earth_ increases. The ratio of charge to potential difference is a constant, called the _capacitance_ of the object. A device that is designed to have a specific _capacitance_ is called a capacitor. A capacitor is used to store _charge_. In the capacitor there are two _conductors_ separated by a(n) _insulator_. The conductors have equal and opposite _charges_. Capacitance is _independent_ of the charge placed on the capacitor. The equation used to calculate capacitance is _$C = q/V$_. In this equation, _C_ represents capacitance, _q_ represents the charge on one plate, and _V_ represents the potential difference between the plates. The unit used to measure capacitance is the _farad_. One coulomb per _volt_ is equal to one farad.

DATE ____ PERIOD ____ NAME ____

Fill in the blanks as you study the chapter.

22.1 CURRENT AND CIRCUITS

Producing Electric Current

When two conducting spheres at different potentials are allowed to touch, _charges_ flow from the object at the _higher_ potential to the object at the _lower_ potential. This flow continues until the potentials are _equal_. The flow of _charged_ particles is called an electric current. In some conductors, negatively charged _electrons_ move. In other conductors, positively charged _particles_ move. To keep the flow of charges moving, there must be a(n) _potential_ difference, which can be maintained by pumping _charges_ from one conductor to another. The pumping process would increase the electric _potential_ energy of the particles, so it would require a(n) _external_ source of energy. A voltaic cell converts _chemical_ energy to electric energy. A photovoltaic cell converts _light_ energy into electric energy. A generator converts _kinetic_ energy into electric energy.

Electric Circuits

A(n) _closed_ loop through which charges move is called an electric circuit. The circuit includes a charge pump that _increases_ the potential energy of the charges, and a device that _reduces_ the potential energy of the charges. This device converts _electric_ energy to another form of energy. A motor converts electric energy to _kinetic_ energy. A lamp converts electric energy to _light_ energy. A heater converts electric energy to _thermal_ energy. Charged particles lose electric _potential energy_ as they flow through such devices, and these devices are said to have _resistance_. The total amount of _charge_ in a circuit does not change, so charge is a(n) _conserved_ quantity. The net change in potential energy of the charges going around the circuit is _zero_.

Rates of Charge Flow and Energy Transfer

The rate at which energy is transferred is _power_. The energy carried by an electric current depends on the _charge_ transferred and the _potential difference_ across which it moves. Electric _current_ is measured in amperes. A device that measures current is called a(n) _ammeter_. The flow of _positive_ charge is called conventional current. The equation used to calculate the power of an electric device is _$P = VI$_. In this equation, _P_ represents power, _V_ represents potential difference, and _I_ represents the current.

CHAPTER 22 Study Guide

NAME ______

Resistance and Ohm's Law

The property that determines how much _current_ will flow in a conductor is resistance. Resistance is measured by placing a potential difference across _two_ points on a conductor, and measuring the _current_ that flows. The equation that defines resistance is $R = \frac{V}{I}$. Resistance is measured in _ohms_. If the resistance of a conductor does not depend on the _size_ or _direction_ of the potential difference across it, the resistance is said to obey _Ohm's_ law. A(n) _resistor_ is a device that is designed to have a specific resistance. A superconductor is a material that has a resistance of _zero_, and can conduct electricity without a(n) _loss_ of energy. Current in a circuit can be controlled by varying either the _potential difference_ or the _resistance_, or both. To produce a smooth, continuous variation in current, a variable _resistor_ called a(n) _potentiometer_ is used.

Diagramming Circuits

A circuit _diagram_, or schematic, is drawn using standard _symbols_ to represent the elements of the _circuit_. When a schematic is drawn, the symbol for the source of electric energy is drawn so that the _positive_ terminal is at the top. A wire following the _conventional_ current is drawn out of this terminal, and the path is followed until the _negative_ terminal of the source of energy is reached. An ammeter is connected to a circuit in a(n) _series_ connection and a voltmeter is connected in a(n) _parallel_ connection.

CHAPTER 22 Study Guide

NAME ______

22.2 USING ELECTRICAL ENERGY

Energy Transfer in Electric Circuits

A capacitor is used to _store_ electric energy. When the capacitor is uncharged, the potential difference across it is _zero_. If a capacitor is connected to a battery through a resistor, _charges_ will flow to the _capacitor_. At first the current will be _large_, but as the voltage across the capacitor increases, the current will _decrease_ until the voltage across the capacitor is _equal to_ the voltage across the battery. At this point the capacitor is _charged_. The capacitor discharges when it is connected across a(n) _resistor_. Current will flow until the voltage across the capacitor is _zero_. The electric energy stored in the capacitor is changed to _thermal_ energy at the resistor. Electric power is the energy per unit _time_ converted by an electric _circuit_ into another form of energy. The equation used to calculate power is $P = I^2R$. If all the electric energy is converted into thermal energy, the energy transferred is the product of _power_ and _time_. The equation used to calculate the increase in thermal energy is $E = I^2Rt$.

Transmission of Electric Energy

If electricity is to be transmitted over long distances, there will be a _loss_ of energy as electric energy is converted to _thermal_ energy. To reduce this loss, there is little that can be done to reduce the _resistance_ of the wires. However, it is possible to reduce the _current_ by increasing the _voltage_.

The Kilowatt Hour

The electric energy used by a device is the product of its _power_ and the _time_ it is operated. The joule is equal to one _watt_ of power per _second_, and is a very small unit. The unit more commonly used is the _kilowatt hour_. If 1000 watts of power are delivered continuously for one hour, one _kilowatt hour_ of energy is used.

DATE ______ PERIOD ______ NAME ______________________

CHAPTER 23 Study Guide

Fill in the blanks as you study the chapter.

23.1 SIMPLE CIRCUITS

Series Circuits

In a series circuit, resistors are connected so that all __current__ flows through each resistor. There is only one __path__ for the current in the circuit. The current in each device is __equal to__ the current in the generator. The increase in potential energy across the __generator__ is equal to the total potential drop, which is equal to the __sum__ of the potential drops around the rest of the circuit. The total resistance, or __equivalent__ resistance, is the __sum__ of the individual resistances in the circuit. The equivalent resistance in a series circuit is __greater than__ the resistance of any one device in the circuit. After the total resistance and total voltage drops have been found, the current in the circuit can be found using the equation $I = \frac{V}{R}$.

Voltage Drops in a Series Circuit

The battery or generator in a circuit __increases__ the potential and the resistors __decrease__ the potential. These two changes are __equal__, and the net change around the circuit is __zero__. The potential drop across any one resistor in a series circuit is determined by finding the __equivalent resistance__ in the circuit and using this to find the current. Once the current is known, this value and the resistance of the individual device are __multiplied__ to find the potential drop across the device. A voltage divider is a simple __series__ circuit that uses an extra __resistor__ to adjust the potential in the circuit.

Parallel Circuits

A parallel circuit has __more than__ one path for the current. The total current is the __sum__ of the currents moving through each path. The potential difference across one of the paths is __equal to__ the potential difference across the other paths. Each path acts as if the other paths __were not__ present. In a parallel circuit, the equivalent resistance is __less than__ the resistance of any individual resistor. If you add another resistor in parallel, the equivalent resistance __decreases__. The reciprocal of the equivalent resistance is equal to the __sum__ of the reciprocals of the individual resistors.

CHAPTER 23 Study Guide

NAME ______________________

23.2 APPLICATIONS OF CIRCUITS

Safety Devices

Fuses and circuit breakers are __switches__ that are used as safety devices that prevent a current __overload__. Most homes use __parallel__ circuits. If several appliances are in use at once, the resistance of each appliance __decreases__ the total resistance of the circuit, which __increases__ the current. The current in an appliance is found by using the equation $I = \frac{P}{V}$. In this equation, P represents the power rating in __watts__, which is marked on the appliance. Once the current is known, the resistance of each appliance can be calculated, using the equation $R = \frac{V}{I}$. After the __equivalent__ resistance for all appliances has been calculated, the total current can be found. If the total current is __greater than__ the rating of the fuse, the fuse will open the circuit. A short circuit occurs when a circuit with a very low __resistance__ forms. Such a circuit carries a very high __current__, which could produce enough __heat__ to start a fire.

Combined Series-Parallel Circuits

The first step in analyzing a combined circuit is to calculate the __equivalent__ resistance of all resistors that are connected in __parallel__. If any of the equivalent resistances are now connected in __series__, calculate their equivalent resistance. Repeat these two steps until the entire circuit has been reduced to __one__ equivalent resistance. Next, calculate the __current__ in the circuit. Finally, calculate the __voltage drops__ and currents through individual resistors.

Ammeters and Voltmeters

An ammeter measures the __current__ in a part of a circuit, and should be connected in __series__ with the resistance. An ammeter should not change the __current__ of the circuit, so it should have the lowest possible __resistance__. A voltmeter measures the __potential drop__ across some part of a circuit, and should be connected in __parallel__ with the resistor. A voltmeter should not change the __current__ or __potential drop__ in a circuit, so it should have a high __resistance__.

DATE ________ PERIOD ________ NAME ____________________

CHAPTER 24 Study Guide

Fill in the blanks as you study the chapter.

24.1 MAGNETS: PERMANENT AND TEMPORARY

General Properties of Magnets

Each end of a magnet is called a(n) __pole__. The north-seeking end of a magnet is the __north__ pole and the south-seeking end of a magnet is the __south__ pole. Two like magnetic poles __repel__ each other and two unlike magnetic poles __attract__ each other. If an object becomes polarized when it is near a magnet, the object has become a(n) __temporary__ magnet. The direction of __polarization__ of a temporary magnet depends on the polarization of the __permanent__ magnet. When the permanent magnet is taken away from the temporary magnet, the temporary magnet will __lose__ its magnetism.

Magnetic Fields Around Permanent Magnets

The forces between magnets occur when the magnets __touch__ each other and when they are at a(n) __distance__. Iron filings can show the __magnetic field__ around a magnet because each filing that is near the magnet becomes a(n) __magnet__. The filing rotates until it is __tangent__ to the magnetic field at that point. Magnetic field lines can be used to show the __strength__ of a magnetic field. The number of magnetic field lines passing through a surface is the __magnetic flux__. The __flux__ per unit area is proportional to the __strength__ of the magnetic field. The flux lines are most concentrated near the __poles__ of the magnet. The direction of the field lines is the direction to which the __N-pole__ of a compass points when it is placed in the field. Magnetic field lines do not have ends, so they form __loops__. The field lines between two __unlike__ poles run directly between the poles. The magnetic field of one magnet can exert a(n) __force__ on a second magnet, causing it to become __aligned__ with the field. When a sample of iron is placed near a magnet, the field lines are __concentrated__ in the sample of iron. The end of the iron sample nearest the N-pole of the magnet becomes the __S-pole__ of the sample, and the sample __attracts__ the magnet. A superconductor __repels__ a magnet because there is no __magnetic flux__ inside the superconductor.

Electromagnetism

When current flows through a wire, it exerts __forces__ on the poles of a magnet in a direction that is __perpendicular to__ the direction of the current. When there is no current flowing in the wire, no __force__ is exerted on a magnet. The magnetic field lines around a wire that is carrying current form a pattern of __concentric__ circles, with the __wire__ at the center of each circle. The strength of the magnetic field around a long, straight wire is proportional to the __current__ in the wire. The strength varies __inversely__

with the distance from the wire. When the direction of current is reversed, the __direction__ of the magnetic field is reversed. According to the first right-hand rule, if your __thumb__ points in the direction of the conventional current, the fingers of your hand circle the __wire__ and point in the __direction__ of the magnetic field.

Magnetic Field Near a Coil

When a current flows through a coil of wire, the field around all the loops will have the same __direction__. The field around the coil is similar to the field around a(n) __permanent magnet__, and the coil has a(n) __north__ pole and a(n) __south__ pole. Because the coil acts like a(n) __magnet__, it is called an electromagnet. According to the second right-hand rule, if your __fingers__ point in the direction of conventional current in the coil, your __thumb__ points toward the N-pole of the electromagnet. The field of an electromagnet becomes __stronger__ when an iron core is placed inside the coil because the core becomes __magnetized__ by induction. The strength of the field around an electromagnet is proportional to the __amount__ of current in the coil and the number of __loops__ in the coil. It also depends on the __nature__ of the core.

A Microscopic Picture of Magnetic Materials

Magnetism in a permanent magnet is the result of the magnetic fields of __electrons__. The fields of groups of atoms called __domains__ act together. If a piece of iron is not magnetized, the domains point in __random__ directions, and their fields __cancel__ each other. A magnetic field causes the domains to __align__ with the field. If the domains remain aligned after the magnetic field is removed, the object is a(n) __permanent__ magnet. If the domains lose their alignment, the object is a(n) __temporary__ magnet.

CHAPTER 24 Study Guide

NAME ____________

24.2 FORCES CAUSED BY MAGNETIC FIELDS

Forces on Currents in Magnetic Fields

The force on a wire in a magnetic field is _perpendicular_ to the direction of the magnetic field and also is _perpendicular_ to the direction of the current. According to the third right-hand rule, if your _fingers_ point in the direction of the magnetic field and your _thumb_ points in the direction of the conventional current, the _palm_ of your hand faces in the direction of the force acting on the wire. When the currents in two wires flow in the same direction, the wires _attract_ each other. If the currents flow in opposite directions, the wires _repel_ each other.

Measuring the Force on a Wire Due to a Magnetic Field

The magnitude of the force acting on a current-carrying wire in a magnetic field is proportional to the _strength_ of the field, the amount of _current_ in the wire, and the _length_ of the wire that is in the field. The strength of a magnetic field is called magnetic _induction_, and is measured in _teslas_. One tesla is equivalent to one _newton_ per _ampere-meter_.

Galvanometers

A galvanometer is used to measure very small _currents_. It contains a small coil of _wire_ placed in the strong field of a(n) _permanent_ magnet. Current passing through the loop causes it to _rotate_, which moves a needle in the galvanometer. The amount of rotation of the needle is proportional to the _current_. A galvanometer can be converted to a(n) _ammeter_ if a resistor with less resistance than the galvanometer is connected in _parallel_ with the galvanometer. A galvanometer can be converted to a(n) _voltmeter_ if a resistor, called a multiplier, is connected in _series_ with the galvanometer.

Electric Motors

The force on a(n) _current-carrying_ loop of wire in a magnetic field causes it to _turn_ through 180°. If the current is _reversed_ at the right time, the loop of wire _rotates_. The current is reversed by a device called a split-ring _commutator_. The loops of wire in an electric motor make up the _armature_. The force acting on the armature is proportional to the number of _loops_ of wire and the _length_ of wire in each loop. The force also is proportional to the amount of _current_ in the wire, and this variable can be used to change the _speed_ of the motor.

The Force on a Single Charged Particle

Charged particles can move in wires and also in any region from which the _air_ has been removed. In a cathode-ray tube, _electric fields_ pull electrons off atoms in the _negative_ electrode. Then electric fields gather, _accelerate_, and focus the electrons into a narrow _beam_, which is deflected by _magnetic fields_. When the electron beam strikes the screen, _phosphors_ on the screen glow, producing an image. The force exerted on an electron by a magnetic field depends on the _velocity_ of the electron, the _strength_ of the field, and the _angle_ between the directions of the velocity and the field.

DATE ________ PERIOD ________ NAME ____________

CHAPTER 25 Study Guide

Fill in the blanks as you study the chapter.

25.1 CREATING ELECTRIC CURRENT FROM CHANGING MAGNETIC FIELDS

Faraday's Discovery

If a wire that is part of a closed _loop_ moves in one direction through a magnetic field, current flows in _one_ direction. If the wire moves in the opposite direction, the _current_ moves in the opposite direction. No current flows if the wire is held _stationary_ or moved _parallel to_ the magnetic field. To produce a current there must be _relative_ motion between the wire and the magnetic field. The process of generating a(n) _current_ in a wire in a(n) _magnetic_ field is electromagnetic induction.

Electromotive Force

The potential difference, or _voltage_, given to charges by a charge pump is called the electromotive _force_. The _volt_ is the unit used to measure *EMF*. When a wire is moved through a magnetic field, a(n) _force_ acts on electrons, which move in the _direction_ of the force. Because _work_ is done on the electrons, their _potential_ energy is increased. The difference in potential is the _induced_ *EMF*. If a wire moves through a field at an angle to the field, only the component of the motion that is _perpendicular to_ the direction of the field generates *EMF*.

Electric Generators

The electric generator converts _mechanical_ energy to electric energy. The generator consists of wire _loops_ placed in a strong _magnetic_ field. The wire is wound around a core of _iron_, and together these parts are called the _armature_. When the armature turns in the field, the wire loops cut through the magnetic field _lines_, and induce an *EMF*, commonly called _voltage_. If the number of loops on the armature is increased, the *EMF* is _increased_. As the loop rotates, the _strength_ and _direction_ of the current change. Each time the loop turns through _180°_, the current reverses direction. A motor is like a generator, but the energy conversion is in the _opposite_ direction, changing electric energy to _mechanical_ energy.

Alternating Current Generator

A(n) _energy_ source turns the armature of a generator in a(n) _magnetic_ field a fixed number of revolutions per second. In the United States, the current changes through a full cycle _60_ times each second, giving the current a frequency of _60 Hz_. The power produced by a generator is the product of the _current_ and the _voltage_. Because these quantities vary, power varies, and is usually described in terms of the _average_ power. The voltage available at electric outlets is the _effective_ voltage, not the _maximum_ voltage.

CHAPTER 25 Study Guide

NAME ______________________

25.2 EFFECTS OF CHANGING MAGNETIC FIELDS: INDUCED *EMF*

Lenz's Law

According to Lenz's law, the __direction__ of the induced current is such that the magnetic field resulting from the induced current opposes the change in __flux__ that caused the induced current. As a result, a generator that is producing __current__ is subject to a force that opposes the turning of the __armature__ of the generator. As the current being generated increases, the magnitude of the opposing force __increases__. In a motor, a similar effect produces __back-*EMF*__, which is in the opposite direction to the flow of current. A mechanical load placed on the motor __decreases__ the net current flowing through the motor, and __decreases__ the back-*EMF*.

Self-Inductance

Current generates a(n) __magnetic__ field, creating new field __lines__, which cut through the wires. As a result, an *EMF* is generated and it opposes the current __change__. The faster you try to change the current, the __larger__ the opposing *EMF*, and the __slower__ the current change. Because of this self-inductance, __work__ has to be done to increase the __current__ that flows, and __energy__ is stored in the magnetic field.

Transformers

A transformer is used to increase or decrease AC __voltages__ without a loss of __energy__. A transformer contains two __coils__ that are insulated electrically from each other, but that share the same __core__. When the primary coil is connected to a source of AC __voltage__, the changing current creates a varying __magnetic__ field. A varying __current__ is induced in the secondary coil, by the process of __mutual__ inductance. The ratio of the primary and secondary __voltages__ depends on the ratio of the number of turns in the two __coils__. In a step-up transformer, the primary voltage is __less than__ the secondary voltage, and the current in the primary circuit is __greater than__ the current in the secondary. In a step-down transformer, the primary voltage is __greater than__ the secondary voltage and the current in the primary circuit is __less than__ the current in the secondary circuit.

DATE ________ PERIOD ________ NAME ______________________

CHAPTER 26 Study Guide

Fill in the blanks as you study the chapter.

26.1 ACTION OF ELECTRIC AND MAGNETIC FIELDS ON MATTER

Mass of the Electron

The mass of an electron can be calculated from the ratio of __charge__ to __mass__. In a cathode-ray tube, crossed __electric__ and __magnetic__ fields exert forces on electrons. The forces exerted by the two fields act in __opposite__ directions. The electric field deflects electrons upward, and the magnetic field deflects electrons __downward__. The electrons travel in a straight line when the forces due to the fields are equal in __magnitude__ and opposite in __direction__. When the electric field is turned off, the magnetic field causes a(n) __centripetal__ acceleration on the electrons, and the electrons are deflected off the straight path. The amount of deflection indicates the charge-to-mass __ratio__. If the electric field is reversed, the same process can be used to find the mass of __positively-charged__ particles.

The Mass Spectrometer

In a mass spectrometer, gas ions with a(n) __positive__ charge are produced. A(n) __electric__ field accelerates the ions, which pass through deflecting __electric__ and __magnetic__ fields. The ions strike a piece of __photographic__ film. Each __isotope__ of the element makes a mark in a different spot on the film. Because all of the ions in the spectrometer have the same charge, the difference in deflection is due to differences in the __mass__ of the isotopes. If containers are used in place of the film, the isotopes can be __collected__ and saved.

CHAPTER 26 Study Guide

NAME ______________________

26.2 ELECTRIC AND MAGNETIC FIELDS IN SPACE

Electromagnetic Waves

Changing magnetic fields induce changing _electric_ fields that are made up of closed _loops_. Changing electric fields induce changing _magnetic_ fields, even if there are no _charges_ present. Combined electric and magnetic _fields_ that move through _space_ are called electromagnetic waves. These waves move at the speed of _light_. When an antenna is connected to a source of alternating current, the current generates a(n) _changing_ magnetic field that moves _outward_ from the antenna. The electric and magnetic fields are at _right_ angles to each other and to the _direction_ of the motion of the wave. The electric field is _parallel_ to the direction of the antenna wires.

Production of Electromagnetic Waves

The _frequency_ of the electromagnetic waves can be changed by varying the speed at which the generator is rotated. The frequencies of radio and television waves are _higher_ than the frequencies that can be produced by a turning generator. These frequencies are produced by the combination of a(n) _coil_ and a(n) _capacitor_. The frequency depends on the _size_ of the capacitor and the coil. Both the _magnetic_ field of the coil and the _electric_ field of the capacitor contain _energy_. When the current is large, the magnetic field has the _greatest_ amount of energy, and the capacitor has the _least_ amount of energy. When the current is _zero_, then all the energy is in the electric field of the _capacitor_. As the energy moves between the electric and magnetic fields, _energy_ is added in the form of _voltage_ pulses. These pulses can also be produced by quartz _crystals_, which generate a(n) _EMF_ when they are bent. Quartz crystals are useful because they produce a(n) _constant_ frequency.

Reception of Electromagnetic Waves

When electromagnetic waves strike an antenna, they _accelerate_ electrons in the antenna. This effect is greatest when the antenna is _parallel_ to the direction of the _electric_ fields of the wave. A(n) _EMF_ in the antenna oscillates at the frequency of the electromagnetic wave. If the length of the antenna is _one half_ the wavelength of the wave, the antenna _resonates_. The antenna is connected to a(n) _coil_ and a(n) _capacitor_. The capacitance is adjusted until the frequency of the _circuit_ equals the frequency of the desired wave. In this way, the device will amplify only one _frequency_.

X Rays

X rays are _high frequency_ electromagnetic waves, produced when _electrons_ are accelerated to high speeds. When the high-speed electrons strike matter, their _kinetic_ energies are converted into electromagnetic _waves_. X rays can be produced by _cathode-ray_ tubes. In a television set, the glass front of the tube contains _lead_, which absorbs the X rays.

DATE ________ PERIOD ________ NAME ______________________

CHAPTER 27 Study Guide

Fill in the blanks as you study the chapter.

27.1 WAVES BEHAVE LIKE PARTICLES

Radiation From Incandescent Bodies

An incandescent object gives off light of all _colors_ as well as _infrared_ radiation. A spectrum is a plot of the _intensity_ of radiation emitted at various _frequencies_. Light and radiation are produced by the _vibrations_ of _charged_ particles within atoms of a hot body. The _frequency_ at which the maximum amount of light is emitted is proportional to the temperature on the _Kelvin_ scale. The total power emitted increases with _temperature_. Max Planck assumed that atoms could vibrate only at specific _frequencies_, and that the energy of vibration is _quantized_. Planck also suggested that an atom could emit radiation only when the vibration energy _changed_.

Photoelectric Effect

The emission of _electrons_ when electromagnetic _radiation_ falls on an object is called the photoelectric effect. The emission of electrons causes a(n) _current_ to flow in a circuit. Electrons are emitted only if the _frequency_ of the radiation is above a minimum value, or _threshold_ frequency. Radiation of a frequency below the threshold value does not _eject_ any electrons from a metal. Once the threshold frequency is reached, the greater the _intensity_ of radiation, and the larger the flow of photoelectrons. Light and other forms of radiation consist of photons, which are discrete bundles of _energy_. The energy of the photon depends on the _frequency_ of the light. To eject an electron, a photon must have a minimum amount of _energy_. If the photon has more than the minimum amount of energy, the excess energy becomes the _kinetic_ energy of the _electron_. The threshold frequency is related to the energy needed to free the most _weakly-bound_ electron from a metal. This amount of energy is called the _work_ function of the metal.

The Compton Effect

Although it has no _mass_, a photon has _kinetic_ energy just as a particle does. Einstein predicted that the photon should have a second particle property, _momentum_. The momentum of a photon is _inversely_ proportional to the wavelength. Arthur Compton found that some X rays lose _energy_ when they strike matter and are scattered with _longer_ wavelengths than the original X rays. The increase in _wavelength_ when X rays are scattered off of _electrons_ is called the Compton effect. Compton also showed that photons obey the law of _conservation_ of momentum and conservation of _energy_.

CHAPTER 27 Study Guide

NAME ______________________

27.2 PARTICLES BEHAVE LIKE WAVES

Matter Waves

Particles such as _electrons_ or protons show wavelike _properties_. If a beam of _electrons_ is aimed at a crystal, the atoms in the crystal act as a(n) _diffraction grating_. The diffraction of the electrons forms the same pattern as diffraction of _X rays_ of a similar wavelength. The wavelength of a particle is the _de Broglie_ wavelength, and is too _small_ to produce observable effects.

Particles and Waves

A(n) _particle_ is usually described in terms of mass, size, kinetic energy, and momentum. A(n) _wave_ is usually described in terms of frequency, wavelength, and amplitude. Because of its length, a wave cannot be located at one _point_ in space. Most scientists believe that the particle and wave aspects of light should be studied _together_. To find the location of a(n) _particle_, light must be reflected from it. The spreading out of light due to _diffraction_ makes it impossible to locate a particle exactly. If light of a(n) _shorter_ wavelength is used, there is less diffraction. However, because of the _Compton_ effect, the short-wavelength light changes the _momentum_ of the particle. Thus, measuring the _position_ of a particle changes its momentum. Similarly, measuring the momentum changes the _position_ of the particle. As a result, the _momentum_ and _position_ of a particle cannot be precisely known at the same _time_. This statement is the Heisenberg _uncertainty_ principle, which is the result of the _dual_ wave and particle description of light and _matter_.

DATE __________ PERIOD __________ NAME ______________________

CHAPTER 28 Study Guide

Fill in the blanks as you study the chapter.

28.1 THE BOHR MODEL

The Nuclear Model

Rutherford probed _atoms_ with massive, high-speed particles that had a(n) _positive_ charge. These particles are now called _alpha_ particles. Rutherford aimed these particles at a thin sheet of metal, and found that _most_ of the particles passed through the sheet. A few of the particles were deflected at _large_ angles. These results are explained by the fact that the nucleus of an atom contains nearly all the _mass_ of the atom. All of the _positive_ charge is also in the nucleus. _Electrons_ are outside the nucleus, and the atom is made up mostly of _empty space_.

Atomic Spectra

The set of wavelengths of light emitted by an atom is the atom's _emission_ spectrum. When a substance is vaporized in a flame it gives off light that is characteristic of the atoms of the _elements_ that make up the substance. Atoms in a gas at low _pressure_ emit light when a high _voltage_ is applied across the gas. The spectrum can be studied through a(n) _diffraction_ grating. The spectrum can also be studied with a(n) _spectroscope_, in which light passes through a(n) _slit_, then a grating, and then a lens system. The spectrum of a(n) _incandescent_ solid is a continuous band of colors. The spectrum of a(n) _gas_ is a series of bright lines, one for each _wavelength_ of light given off by the atoms in the gas. When light passes through a gas that is cool, the gas will _absorb_ light at characteristic _wavelengths_, forming a(n) _absorption_ spectrum. The wavelengths that are absorbed by atoms in a cool gas are _the same as_ the wavelengths the atoms give off when they are excited.

The Bohr Model of the Atom

Rutherford described an atom in which _electrons_ orbited the nucleus much as planets orbit the _sun_. This planetary model did not account for the fact that no radiation is _emitted_ as electrons move around the nucleus. It also did not account for the fact that atoms emit light only at specific _wavelengths_. Bohr suggested that an electron in a stable orbit does not radiate _energy_, even though the electron is _accelerating_. Light is emitted when the _energy_ of an electron changes. An electron can absorb only certain amounts of _energy_. Thus the energy of an electron in an atom is _quantized_. The different amounts of energy that an electron can have are the energy _levels_, the lowest of which is the _ground_ state. If an electron absorbs _energy_, it moves to a(n) _excited_ state. This condition lasts a very short time, and the electron returns to the _ground_ state. During this change, the electron emits a(n) _photon_.

NAME ______

Predictions of the Bohr Model

The Bohr model correctly predicted the _emission_ spectrum for the element _hydrogen_, but not for the next element, _helium_. In his model, Bohr suggested that the angular _momentum_ of an electron can have only certain values. Thus angular momentum is _quantized_. In addition, the radius of a(n) _orbit_ and the _energy_ of the electron can have only certain values, and are _quantized_. The principal _quantum_ number determines the radius of the orbit and energy of the _electron_.

NAME ______

28.2 THE PRESENT MODEL OF THE ATOM

A Quantum Model of the Atom

The quantization of the _angular_ momentum of an electron is related to the fact that particles show some properties of _waves_. Because the _position_ and _momentum_ of a particle cannot both be known at the same time, the quantum model of the atom predicts only the _probability_ that an electron is at a given location. The region in which there is a(n) _high_ probability of finding an electron is the electron _cloud_. This model is the basis for quantum _mechanics_, which allows scientists to determine the structure of atoms and _molecules_.

Lasers

Because the light emitted by a(n) _incandescent_ source is at many wavelengths and moving in all directions, the light is described as _incoherent_. When an atom in an excited state is struck by a photon with the correct amount of _energy_, the atom will emit another photon. The two photons will have the same _wavelength_ and will be in step with each other. In a laser, a flash of light with a(n) _shorter_ wavelength than that of the laser is used to excite _atoms_. As the atoms decay to a(n) _lower_ state, they lase, or give off _light_. As photons are produced, they strike other _atoms_, which then give off more _photons_. The photons are trapped inside a tube and only a few photons leave through a _partially_ reflecting mirror. Because all the photons are in step, laser light is described as _coherent_. Because the beam is small, the light is also very _intense_. The light is all one wavelength, or _monochromatic_. Laser light can be carried through glass fibers because the light undergoes total _internal reflection_.

DATE ________ PERIOD ________ NAME ____________________

CHAPTER 29 Study Guide

Fill in the blanks as you study the chapter.

29.1 CONDUCTION IN SOLIDS

Band Theory of Solids

In a(n) __conductor__, electrical charges can move easily. In a(n) __insulator__, charges remain where they are placed. In a single atom, electrons are usually in the __lowest__ possible energy level. When atoms are brought together, their individual __electric__ fields affect each other, and change the __energy__ levels. In one atom the energy levels are raised, and in the other atom they are __lowered__. When many atoms are together in a(n) __solid__ object, no two atoms have the __same__ energy levels. The many levels are spread into __bands__, which are separated by values that are called __forbidden gaps__ because atoms are not allowed to have these energies. In conductors, the __lowest__ band is only partially filled.

Conductors

When a potential difference is placed across a material, the resulting __electric__ field exerts a(n) __force__ on electrons. The electrons are __accelerated__ and they gain __energy__. This change allows them to move into a(n) __higher__ energy level. In conductors, the bands are only __partially__ filled, so there is a higher level into which the electrons can move. As electrons gain energy from the electric __field__, they move from one __atom__ to the next. The free electrons in a conductor move __rapidly__ in __random__ directions. An electric field placed across a conductor exerts a(n) __force__ on the electrons, which still move __randomly__, but drift toward the __positive__ end of the conductor. This description of a conductor is the __electron gas__ model. If the temperature is increased, the speed of the electrons __increases__, but the electrons are more likely to __collide__ with a nucleus. As a result, an increase in temperature causes a decrease in __conductivity__ and an increase in __resistance__.

Insulators

In an insulator, all energy levels in the __lower__ band are filled. The next available energy level is in a(n) __higher__ band. If an electron is to be moved through an insulator, it must receive enough energy to remove it from the lowest, or __valence__, band. Most electric fields do not have enough energy to move electrons from this band to the __conduction__ band. In an insulator, the __forbidden__ gap between the bands is very __wide__, and few electrons can be moved across it.

Semiconductors

In a semiconductor, electrons move __more__ freely than in insulators, but __less__ freely than in conductors. Most semiconductors have __four__ valence electrons, which are involved in __binding__ atoms into a crystal structure. The valence electrons fill a(n) __band__ but the __forbidden gap__ between the valence

CHAPTER 29 Study Guide NAME ____________________

and conduction bands is smaller than it is in a(n) __insulator__. Very little __energy__ is needed to move an electron into the __conduction__ band. As the temperature of the semiconductor increases, __more__ electrons are moved into the conduction band. In a semiconductor, as temperature increases, __conductivity__ increases. An atom from which a(n) __electron__ has broken free contains a hole, or an empty __energy__ level in the __valence__ band. The hole has a(n) __positive__ charge, and a(n) __electron__ can move into it. Although this hole is filled, the electron that filled it leaves behind a(n) __hole__ in another atom. The electrons and the holes move in __opposite__ directions. A semiconductor that develops holes because of __thermal__ energy is a(n) __intrinsic__ semiconductor, and has a low conductivity and a high __resistance__.

Doped Semiconductors

The conductivity of a semiconductor can be increased if impurities called __extrinsic__ semiconductors are added. These dopants add extra __electrons__ or __holes__ to the semiconductor. If an atom with five valence electrons replaces an atom with four valence electrons, there is __one__ electron that is not needed in __bonding__. This extra, or __donor__ electron can be moved into the conduction band by a small amount of __thermal__ energy. The semiconductor that conducts by means of __electrons__ is called a(n) __n-type__ semiconductor because it conducts by particles with a(n) __negative__ charge. If an atom with three valence electrons replaces an atom with four, an extra __hole__ is formed. Because an electron can move into the hole, the atom is called an electron __acceptor__. This type of semiconductor is called a(n) __p-type__ semiconductor. In either type of semiconductor, the net charge on the semiconductor is __zero__.

CHAPTER 29 Study Guide

NAME ______

29.2 ELECTRONIC DEVICES

Diodes

A diode consists of adjacent regions of _p-type_ and _n-type_ semiconductors. The boundary between the two regions is called the _junction_. Charges move until the n-side has a net _negative_ charge, and the p-side has a net _positive_ charge. Forces between these charges stop the movement of charges in the _depletion_ layer. If the n-type end of a diode is connected to the positive terminal of a battery, both free electrons and holes are attracted toward the battery and the depletion layer is _increased_. In this reverse-biased diode there is a very large _resistance_ and a very _small_ current. If the battery is connected in the opposite way, charge carriers move toward the _junction_ in the diode, making the _depletion_ layer smaller, and current flows. This forward-biased diode can be used to change _AC_ current to current with only one _polarity_. When electrons reach the holes at the junction in _light-emitting_ diodes, or LEDs, the excess _energy_ is released as light. If the semiconductor crystal is shaped in such a way that light reflects inside the crystal, the diode becomes a(n) _laser_. A reverse-biased diode can be used as a light _detector_.

Transistors and Integrated Circuits

In a transistor, there are _three_ layers of doped _semiconductors_. The _central_ layer, or base, is different from the two outer layers, which are called the _emitter_ and the _collector_. In an npn transistor, the potential difference between the collector and emitter is _positive_. The base-collector junction acts as a(n) _reverse-biased_ diode, so no current flows. The base-emitter junction acts as a(n) _forward-biased_ diode. A small current through the base-emitter junction produces a(n) _large_ current through the base-collector junction. The transistor increases, or _amplifies_, voltage changes. In a pnp resistor, the battery potentials are _reversed_, and current is carried by _holes_.

DATE ______ PERIOD ______ NAME ______

CHAPTER 30 Study Guide

Fill in the blanks as you study the chapter.

30.1 RADIOACTIVITY

Description of the Nucleus

The _positive_ charge of an atom is found in the nucleus. The positively-charged particle found in the _nucleus_ of an atom is the _proton_. The mass of the proton is _one_ atomic mass unit. The number of protons in the nucleus is the atom's atomic _number_. All atoms of a given element have the same number of _protons_. The mass of a nucleus is _greater than_ the combined masses of the protons. The neutron is a particle found in the _nucleus_. This particle has _no_ charge and has a mass about equal to the mass of one _proton_. The sum of the _protons_ and _neutrons_ in a nucleus is the mass number. In elements with 20 or fewer protons, the number of protons is about _equal to_ the number of neutrons. In elements with more than 20 protons the number of protons is generally _less than_ than the number of neutrons.

Isotopes

Atoms with the same _atomic_ number but different _mass_ numbers are isotopes of the same element. The nucleus of an isotope is called a(n) _nuclide_. When a sample of an element is analyzed in a mass _spectrometer_, there is _one_ spot on the film for each isotope. All isotopes of an element have the same number of _electrons_ around the nucleus, and have the same _chemical_ behavior. The notation for isotopes involves a superscript and a subscript, both of which are written to the _left_ of the _symbol_ for the element. The _atomic_ number is the subscript and the _mass_ number is the superscript.

Radioactive Decay

Nuclei that decay are described as _radioactive_. Rutherford identified _three_ kinds of radiation. Two of the forms, _alpha_ and _beta_, are charged particles. Gamma radiation is made up of high-energy _photons_. The release of an alpha particle causes a nucleus to lose _two_ charge units and _four_ mass units. The element has been changed, or _transmuted_, into a different element. Beta particles are high-speed _electrons_, and have a(n) _negative_ charge. In beta decay, the _atomic_ number increases by one and the _mass_ number does not change. Gamma radiation results from the redistribution of _charge_ in the nucleus. Gamma radiation does not change the _atomic_ number or the _mass_ number.

Nuclear Reactions and Equations

A nuclear reaction occurs whenever the number of __neutrons__ or __protons__ in the nucleus changes. The emission of particles from a(n) __radioactive__ nucleus releases energy in the form of __kinetic__ energy of the emitted particles. The nuclear reaction does not destroy any __particles__. In a nuclear reaction, electric charge is __conserved__.

Half-Life

The time required for __one-half__ of the atoms in a sample of radioactive isotope to __decay__ is the half-life of that isotope. The number of decays per __second__ is the activity of the substance. Activity is __proportional__ to the number of radioactive atoms present. The activity is reduced by __one-half__ during one half-life of the sample.

30.2 THE BUILDING BLOCKS OF MATTER

Nuclear Bombardment

Rutherford used __alpha__ particles to cause nuclear reactions. As a result, high-speed __neutrons__ were released by nuclei. Because neutrons are __uncharged__, they are not repelled by a nucleus, which makes them useful in bombarding nuclei. One of the problems with using alpha particles is that they have __fixed__ energies, and need to be artificially __accelerated__ to higher energies.

Linear Accelerators

A linear accelerator is a series of hollow __tubes__ in a long __evacuated__ chamber. Protons are produced and accelerated into a tube that has a(n) __negative__ potential. Alternating charges produce __electric__ fields between tubes, which __accelerate__ the protons along the path. Both __protons__ and __electrons__ can be accelerated in a linear accelerator.

The Synchrotron

A synchrotron uses __magnetic__ fields to move charged particles in __circular__ paths. In between the magnets, there are regions in which high-frequency alternating __voltage__ accelerates the particles. In a synchrotron it is possible to send particles in two directions so that they will __collide__.

Particle Detectors

Photographic __film__ becomes "fogged" when exposed to radiation. High-speed particles ionize matter, and remove __electrons__ from atoms. Some substances __fluoresce__ when exposed to radiation, and this light can be used to detect radiation. In a Geiger-Mueller tube, particles ionize __gas__ atoms. The positive particle is accelerated toward the cylinder with the __negative__ charge. The negative particle is accelerated toward the wire with the __positive__ charge. As the charged particles strike and ionize other particles they create a pulse of __current__ in the tube. In a cloud chamber, particles leave a trail of __ions__ on which water vapor __condenses__. A(n) __spark__ chamber is like a huge Geiger-Mueller tube. Because a(n) __neutral__ particle does not produce a discharge, laws of conservation of __energy__ and __momentum__ are used to see if these particles were part of any collisions.

The Fundamental Particles

The two families of particles of which matter is made are __quarks__ and __leptons__. Protons and neutrons are made up of __quarks__. The electron is a(n) __lepton__. Some additional particles transmit __force__ between particles. The electromagnetic force is carried by the __photon__. The binding forces in the nuclei are carried by __gluons__. The __weak bosons__ are involved in weak interaction, which operates in __beta__ decay. Although the particle that carries __gravitational__ force has not been detected, it is called the __graviton__. Antiparticles are identical to particles except for having the __opposite__ charge. When a particle and its antiparticle collide they __annihilate__ each other and are transformed into __photons__, or lighter particle-antiparticle pairs and __energy__. The total number of quarks and leptons in the universe is __constant__. Quarks and leptons are __created__ and __destroyed__ only in particle-antiparticle pairs.

Particles and Antiparticles

The energy released when a neutron decays is shared by the __beta particle__ and __antineutrino__ that are produced. The antineutrino has __zero__ mass and no charge, but it carries __momentum__ and energy. Emission of a positron is similar to __beta__ decay. A proton changes into a(n) __neutron__ and emits a positron and a(n) __neutrino__. When a positron and a(n) __electron__ collide, they annihilate each other, producing __gamma__ rays. In this process, matter is converted into __energy__. Energy can be converted into __matter__ by a process called __pair__ production. If a gamma ray with enough energy passes close to a(n) __nucleus__, a positron and a(n) __electron__ are formed. If the gamma ray has more than the minimum amount of energy, the extra energy goes into the __kinetic__ energy of the positron and electron.

The Quark Model of Nucleons

The proton and the __neutron__ are made up of quarks. A proton is made up of two __up__ quarks and one __down__ quark. A neutron is made up of one __up__ quark and two __down__ quarks. The force that holds quarks together becomes __stronger__ as the quarks are pulled farther apart. Weak bosons are involved in __beta__ decay. In this process, one __down__ quark in a neutron changes to a(n) __up__ quark, and one __W^- boson__ is emitted. Then this boson decays into an electron and a(n) __antineutrino__. Bombardment of particles at high __energies__ creates particles with very __short__ lifetimes. Such particles, made of __quark-antiquark__ pairs, are mesons. Particles made of __three__ quarks are baryons. To account for all the different particles that can be produced in accelerators, a total of __six__ quarks and __six__ leptons are needed.

CHAPTER 31 Study Guide

Fill in the blanks as you study the chapter.

31.1 HOLDING THE NUCLEUS TOGETHER

The Strong Nuclear Force

The strong nuclear force overcomes the mutual repulsion between __protons__ in the nucleus. The force acts over a range about the size of the __radius__ of a proton. The strength of the strong force between two protons is __equal to__ the strength of the strong force between a proton and a neutron. To remove a proton or a neutron from a nucleus, __work__ must be done to overcome the attractive __force__. Doing work increases the __energy__ of a system. This means that the assembled nucleus has __less__ energy than the separate nucleons that make up the nucleus. The difference in energy is the __binding__ energy of the nucleus. Because the nucleus has less energy than its parts, the sign of the binding energy is __negative__.

Binding Energy of the Nucleus

The binding energy of a nucleus is proportional to the difference between the __mass__ of the nucleus and the __masses__ of the nucleons from which it is made. The difference between these two masses is the mass __defect__, which can be determined experimentally. From this value, the __binding__ energy can be calculated. For most nuclei, the binding energy per nucleon becomes more __negative__ as the __mass__ number increases to 56. This isotope of iron has the __most__ tightly-bound nucleus. Nuclei that are smaller or larger are __less__ tightly bound. A nuclear reaction will occur naturally if the reaction releases __energy__. This occurs if the new nucleus is __more__ tightly bound than the original nucleus. When a heavy nucleus decays by the release of an alpha particle, the binding __energy__ per nucleon of the new nucleus is __less__ than that of the original nucleus. The excess energy is transferred into the __kinetic__ energy of the alpha particle. For small nuclei, reactions that __increase__ the number of nucleons in a nucleus make the binding energy more __negative__. Such a reaction occurs on the sun, where the excess energy becomes the __electromagnetic__ radiation that we see as light.

31.2 USING NUCLEAR ENERGY

Artificial Radioactivity

Radioactive isotopes can be formed from stable isotopes if they are bombarded with gamma rays or particles such as alpha particles or neutrons. The unstable nuclei that form emit radiation until they are transmuted into stable isotopes. Artificially-produced isotopes, called tracers, allow doctors to follow the path of molecules in the body. A PET scanner uses isotopes that emit positrons. The scanner identifies gamma rays produced when a(n) electron-positron pair annihilate each other. A computer then makes a three-dimensional map of the distribution of decaying nuclei. Radioactivity is also used as a way to destroy certain cells, as in cancer patients. Unstable particles produced in a particle accelerator can also be used to kill cells.

Nuclear Fission

Nuclear fission is the splitting of a(n) nucleus into two or more fragments of approximately equal size. Such a reaction involves the release of a large amount of energy. Some isotopes of uranium undergo fission when they are bombarded with neutrons. To find the energy released by each fission, write a(n) equation for the reaction and calculate the masses on each side of the equation. The right side of the equation should show less mass than the left side of the equation. This energy equivalent is transferred to the kinetic energy of the fission products. Since fission reactions release neutrons, which can split other uranium atoms, the reaction continues, and is called a(n) chain reaction.

Nuclear Reactors

Most of the neutrons produced in fission are moving at speeds that are too great to cause additional fissions. In a nuclear reactor, the moderator surrounds the uranium fuel and provides light atoms with which fast neutrons will collide. When a neutron collides with a light atom, it transfers momentum and energy to the atom. The neutron then becomes a(n) slow neutron, which can split another uranium nucleus. Graphite and heavy water can be used as moderators in reactors that have as little as 1% ${}^{235}_{92}U$, which is the fissionable isotope. If ordinary water is to be used as a moderator, the amount of this isotope must be increased by a process called enrichment. In the United States, most reactors are pressurized water reactors. In these reactors, water is both the moderator and the coolant, which transfers thermal energy away from the fissioning uranium. In the reactor, rods of a substance, such as cadmium, which can absorb neutrons are used to regulate the rate of the chain reaction. When these control rods are inserted all the way into the reactor, the chain reaction stops. The thermal energy that is released by fission heats water, which flows under pressure to a heat exchanger, where the thermal energy boils water in a separate circuit. The boiling water produces steam, which

turns a(n) turbine. After fission takes place, the fuel rods from the reactor contain radioactive waste products which must be removed and stored in a safe place. There is a limited amount of uranium, so scientists are working on the breeder reactor, which produces more nuclear fuel than it uses.

Nuclear Fusion

Fusion is the union of small nuclei to produce larger ones. The larger nucleus is more tightly bound, so its mass is less than the masses of the smaller nuclei. The energy equivalent of this mass is very large, and is transferred to the kinetic energy of the particles that are formed. In the sun, fusion converts four protons into one helium nucleus. Because fusion requires huge amounts of thermal energy, these reactions are sometimes called thermonuclear reactions.

Controlled Fusion

To confine the fusion reaction in a controlled fusion, magnetic fields are used to hold the plasma, made up of electrons and ions. An increase in the magnetic field can increase the temperature of the plasma, causing hydrogen nuclei to fuse into helium nuclei. The energy released could be used to heat some material which would then boil water to turn a(n) turbine. Currently, fusion reactions use more energy than they produce. Another way to control fusion is to enclose the fuel in tiny glass spheres, and then direct laser beams at them. The pellets then implode, which increases the pressure. The increased pressure increases the temperature to levels needed for fusion to occur.